ECUADOR
in Pictures

Alison Behnke

TF
CB
Twenty-First Century Books

Contents

Lerner Publishing Group, Inc., realizes that current information and statistics quickly become out of date. To extend the usefulness of the Visual Geography Series, we developed www.vgsbooks.com, a website offering links to up-to-date information, as well as in-depth material, on a wide variety of subjects. All of the websites listed on www.vgsbooks.com have been carefully selected by researchers at Lerner Publishing Group, Inc. However, Lerner Publishing Group, Inc., is not responsible for the accuracy or suitability of the material on any website other than www.lernerbooks.com. It is recommended that students using the Internet be supervised by a parent or teacher. Links on www.vgsbooks.com will be regularly reviewed and updated as needed.

INTRODUCTION — 4

THE LAND — 8

► Topography. The Galápagos Islands. Rivers. Climate. Flora and Fauna. Natural Resources and Environmental Challenges. Cities and Towns.

HISTORY AND GOVERNMENT — 20

► Pre-Columbian Era. Under the Inca Empire. Spanish Exploration and Conquest. Colonial Days. Independence. The Early Republic. Changes and Challenges. Ups and Downs. Ongoing Issues. Government.

THE PEOPLE — 36

► Ethnic Groups. Language. Education. Health. Daily Life. Social Issues and Change.

Website address: www.lernerbooks.com

Twenty-First Century Books
A division of Lerner Publishing Group, Inc.
241 First Avenue North
Minneapolis, MN 55401 U.S.A.

0 1021 0233641 3

web enhanced @ www.vgsbooks.com

CULTURAL LIFE 44

► Religion. Holidays and Festivals. Food. Literature. Visual Arts. Music. Sports and Recreation.

THE ECONOMY 56

► Services and Trade. Mining and Industry. Agriculture and Livestock. Fishing and Forestry. Energy. Transportation. Media and Communications. The Future.

FOR MORE INFORMATION

► Timeline	66
► Fast Facts	68
► Currency	68
► Flag	69
► National Anthem	69
► Famous People	70
► Sights to See	72
► Glossary	73
► Selected Bibliography	74
► Further Reading and Websites	76
► Index	78

Library of Congress Cataloging-in-Publication Data

Behnke, Alison.
    Ecuador in pictures / by Alison Behnke.
        p.   cm. — (Visual geography series)
    Includes bibliographical references and index.
    ISBN 978-0-8225-8573-2 (lib. bdg. : alk. paper)
    1. Ecuador—Pictorial works—Juvenile literature. 2. Ecuador—Juvenile literature. I. Title.
F3708.5.B44 2009
986.60022'2—dc22   2008000421

Manufactured in the United States of America
1 2 3 4 5 6 - BP - 14 13 12 11 10 09

INTRODUCTION

The Republic of Ecuador lies on South America's west coast, between Colombia and Peru. The small nation—home to 13.5 million people—has a dramatic landscape rich in natural beauty. Off the nation's western coast lie the Galápagos Islands. This chain of islands is famous worldwide for its unique and precious variety of wildlife. On the mainland, Ecuador's terrain rises from lowlands along the Pacific Ocean, up to the high peaks of the Andes Mountains, and back down to dense jungles marching eastward toward the mighty Amazon River.

Like its natural setting, this small nation's history has had many ups and downs. The region was originally home to a variety of indigenous (native) groups. It came under the control of the powerful Inca Empire in the 1400s. Inca influence was followed by Spanish rule in the 1500s, as Spain colonized much of South and Central America. The Spanish colonists brought new influences, including their language, their religion, and other cultural elements.

The nation achieved its independence from Spanish rule in 1830. But that independence did not bring the Republic of Ecuador easy times. In the following decades, the Ecuadorian government was unstable. It frequently suffered from internal conflict. As the years passed, such shaky governing shattered the public's faith in its leaders. On top of these political troubles, the nation suffered economic challenges.

But a spark of hope remained. For centuries, most of Ecuador's inhabitants had lived in the mountainous highlands—especially near the capital city of Quito—and on the coastal lowlands. Local legend and lore imagined the jungle east of the Andes, called El Oriente (the East), as a place of fabulous wealth. That myth became reality in 1967 when drilling revealed vast petroleum deposits in El Oriente. Ecuador began pumping and exporting oil in the 1970s, tapping into a thriving world oil market. These boom years brought many Ecuadorians increased financial stability and a higher standard of living and made some people very wealthy.

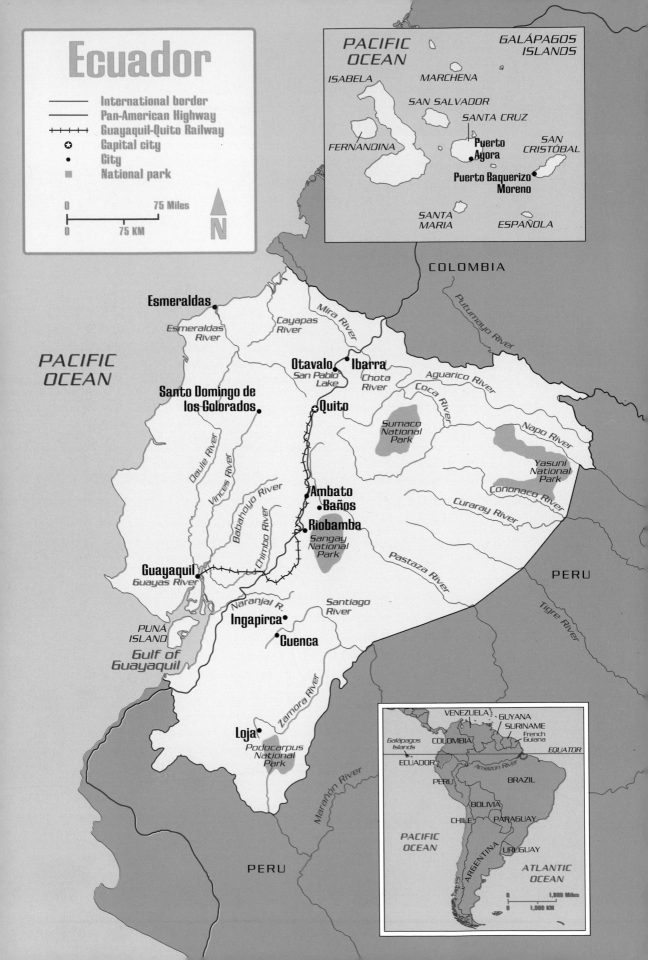

The nation's upward trend turned downward in the 1980s, when oil prices dropped dramatically. The change brought renewed hardships. These in turn led to widespread unrest and dissatisfaction. And while oil had brought prosperity, it had opened Ecuador to strong outside influence once again. The demands and desires of foreign oil investors sometimes clashed with the needs of Ecuador's residents. High poverty rates and inadequate education and health care plagued the country. But few leaders stayed in office long enough to address these issues successfully. And regional relations suffered in March 2008, when Ecuador's neighbor Colombia launched a raid in Ecuadorian territory, targeting a Colombian rebel group.

Nevertheless, the Ecuadorian government has appeared to stabilize. Looking to the future, Ecuadorians are eager to keep strengthening their democracy as well as their economy. Other goals include protecting the country's precious environment, increasing rights and representation for indigenous peoples, and raising the standard of living for all citizens. Ecuadorians hope that, with hard work and good governing, their nation's fortunes will reach new and greater heights.

The Republic of Ecuador takes its name from the Spanish word for the equator, *el ecuador*. The equator—an imaginary line dividing Earth into Northern and Southern Hemispheres—crosses northern Ecuador.

THE LAND

The Republic of Ecuador's territory covers 109,483 square miles (283,560 square kilometers). This area makes it about the same size as the U.S. state of Nevada. Ecuador's neighbor Colombia lies to the north. Peru forms its eastern and southern borders. The Pacific Ocean washes against Ecuador's western border.

Ecuador's territory also includes the Galápagos Islands. The Galápagos archipelago (island group) lies 600 miles (966 km) west of Ecuador's mainland shores. In the 1800s, the British naturalist Charles Darwin studied the Galápagos's rich plant and animal life. The information he gathered there helped him develop his theory of the evolution of life on Earth. Scientists from many nations still visit the islands to study flora and fauna that have evolved under unique and isolated environmental conditions.

◉ Topography

Mainland Ecuador's landscape comprises three major areas. From west to east, these regions are the Costa, the Andes Mountains, and El Oriente.

The Costa—Spanish for "coast"— is a strip of coastal lowlands between the Pacific Ocean and the nation's central mountains. This region ranges from about 15 to 100 miles (24 to 161 km) wide. It is mostly flatland. But near Guayaquil, the nation's biggest city, hills rise out of the plains.

The Costa is very fertile. For thousands of years, rivers have dumped rich volcanic ash in the region's soils. This fertile soil makes the Costa Ecuador's most commercially productive region.

Moving eastward from the Pacific lowlands, Ecuador's land rises toward the Andes. Also called the sierra, this rugged mountainous region makes up about one-quarter of the nation's area.

The Andes Mountains make up the world's longest mountain chain, running almost the entire length of South America. The section that passes through Ecuador is called the Cordillera Real (Royal Range). This range includes two subchains that run north to south, linked in places by horizontal ridges. Towering mountain peaks dot Ecuador's landscape.

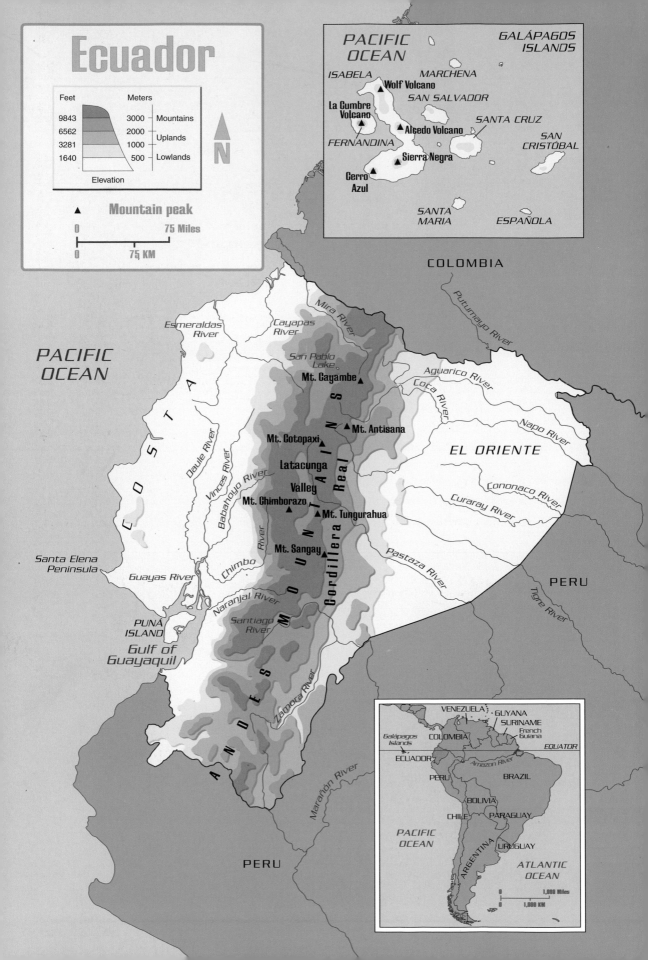

Chimborazo is the highest, at 20,561 feet (6,267 meters) above sea level. The second-tallest is Cotopaxi, rising to 19,347 feet (5,897 m). It is also one of the world's highest active volcanoes. Other notable peaks include Cayambe, Antisana, and Sangay. Between the sierra's chains lie fertile valleys that are home to more than one-half of Ecuador's people.

Ecuador's third region is El Oriente. Its name means "The East" in Spanish. This area begins at the eastern foothills of the Andes and extends to the Amazon River's basin (the area that the river and its branches drain). El Oriente is made up of rain forests, jungles, and rivers. The altitude, or height above sea level, drops rapidly in this easternmost region. Waterfalls and mighty rapids carry water from the cold mountaintops through El Oriente. Lower, at about 850 feet (259 m) above sea level, the land is more level, with tree-cleared land areas

RING OF FIRE

Ecuador is part of a dangerous region called the Ring of Fire. Most of the world's volcanic eruptions and earthquakes occur in this area, which forms a rough circle looping partly around the Pacific Ocean. Ecuador's ruggedly beautiful landscape offers a clue to this fiery nature. The small nation is home to dozens of volcanoes (though not all of them are active). Mount Cotopaxi alone has erupted more than forty-five times since 1738. These eruptions often lead to mudflows that rush down mountainsides. Earthquakes are another danger and have struck Ecuador many times over the years.

The Cotopaxi volcano, Ecuador's second-highest, lies 50 miles (80 km) south of the capital, Quito. It is topped by one of the world's few equatorial glaciers. The extreme altitude of Cotopaxi supports a year-round ice cap even in the tropics. Evidence exists that early Ecuadorian cultures worshipped Cotopaxi.

HABITS OF THE TORTOISE

British naturalist Charles Darwin recorded the activities of the giant tortoises *(below)* living on the Galápagos Islands. Some of his observations follow below.

"The tortoise is very fond of water, drinking large quantities, and wallowing in the mud. The larger islands alone possess springs, and these are always situated towards the central parts, and at a considerable height. The tortoises, therefore, which frequent the lower districts, when thirsty, are obliged to travel from a long distance. Hence broad and well-beaten paths branch off in every direction from the wells down to the sea-coast. . . . Near the springs it was a curious spectacle to behold many of these huge creatures, one set eagerly travelling onwards with outstretched necks, and another set returning, after having drunk their fill. When the tortoise arrives at the spring, quite regardless of any spectator, he buries his head in the water above his eyes, and greedily swallows great mouthfuls."

—Charles Darwin in *The Voyage of the Beagle*, 1838–1843

better suited to farming. But dense forests cover much of the region.

The Galápagos Islands

Early indigenous peoples may have visited the Galápagos Islands, but historians are not sure. The first European to arrive was Spanish explorer Tomás de Berlanga. He happened upon the islands off Ecuador's mainland in 1535. The Spanish first called these volcanic islands Las Islas Encantadas (the Enchanted Islands). They named them for the area's very strong currents, which often fooled navigators. Later the island group became the Galápagos (Spanish for "turtles"), named for the giant tortoises discovered there.

Even before humans lived on the islands, the Galápagos became well known. They were popular with people ranging from pirates who favored them as a hideout to naturalists eager to study their wildlife. Ecuador officially took over the islands in 1832.

In the late 1800s, some people began moving to the islands, and in modern times the Galápagos are home to more than 20,000 people. These residents inhabit five of the fourteen islands. Most live in the two main cities of Puerto Ayora (on the island Santa Cruz) and Puerto Baquerizo Moreno (on the island San Cristóbal).

◉ Rivers

Many streams and rivers crisscross Ecuador. The Guayas River drains the lower western region. Its largest tributaries, or branches, are the Daule, Babahoyo, Chimbo, and Naranjal rivers. Within about 50 miles (80 km), eight rivers empty huge amounts of freshwater into the Pacific Ocean at the Gulf of Guayaquil. The Mira, Cayapas, and Esmeraldas rivers of northwestern Ecuador also flow to the Pacific. A tributary of the Esmeraldas drains the area around the capital city of Quito, in the sierra, and passes through a gorge (narrow canyon) in the Cordillera Real.

South of Quito, the Pastaza River drains the Latacunga Valley. The Pastaza then flows in a southeastward route to the Amazon River. But the Amazon itself lies beyond the nation's borders. Even navigable portions of waterways flowing into the Amazon lie 50 miles (80 km) outside of Ecuador's territory, in neighboring Peru. South of the Pastaza, the Zamora River flows into the Marañón (and later the Amazon).

Major rivers in El Oriente are the Coca, Napo, Curaray, and Cononaco. All of these waterways eventually flow into the Amazon River.

A local fisher travels the Napo River in a dugout canoe. **The Napo eventually drains into the Amazon River in Brazil. Visit www.vgsbooks.com for links to more information about Ecuador's waterways, volcanoes, islands, and more.**

Climate

Tropical countries (countries near the equator) generally have the hottest climates in the world. As in other mountainous tropical regions, however, Ecuador's climate varies considerably with elevation. Rainfall depends on rain-bearing winds, and conditions often change abruptly. For example, while most of the sierra gets plenty of rain, an area just north of Quito receives very little. Southern Ecuador and the Santa Elena Peninsula west of Guayaquil are also quite dry.

The Galápagos Islands and the mainland Costa region are quite warm all year. The Galápagos enjoy average highs of about 81°F (27°C). Like other parts of Ecuador, the islands also have a dry season and a rainy season.

At low elevations along the coast, temperatures average between 75°F (24°C) and 78°F (26°C) all year. Ecuador's northwestern coast tends to be warm and wet for most of the year, while the southwestern coast is drier. Just south of Esmeraldas, the rainy season occurs between January and May, but farther south this season grows shorter. The Peru Current, which flows out of the southern Pacific Ocean from June to December, cools coastal waters and also causes heavy fog.

Farther inland, the climate varies greatly with altitude. The *tierra caliente*, or hot zone, extends from sea level to about 3,000 feet (914

m). Above the tierra caliente, the *tierra templada* (moderately warm region) rises to about 6,500 feet (1,981 m). The next zone up is the *tierra fría*, or cold land, which extends higher than 10,000 feet (3,048 m). Windy, treeless paramos (alpine flatlands) are found still higher. The highest level is the snow line, found at about 15,000 feet (4,572 m) above sea level.

A group of Ecuadorians walks along a rural road near the slopes of **Mount Chimborazo.**

El Oriente has a typically hot equatorial climate, with temperatures that are almost always around 79°F (26°C). But because the region is usually humid, with high moisture levels, it can feel much hotter. Rainfall exceeds 100 inches (254 centimeters) annually in most of El Oriente, and the rain forest sometimes receives more than 200 inches (508 cm) a year. The driest period in the region is November through February.

Within each of these zones, little seasonal variation occurs between the warmest and the coldest months. In Quito, for example, low temperatures average about 50°F (10°C) and highs average approximately 68°F (20°C) year-round.

Flora and Fauna

Ecuador contains a vast array of plant and animal life. Isolated jungles, valleys, islands, and mountains, as well as wide variations of climate, account for the nation's enormous assortment of flora and fauna.

The wet lowlands and rain forests of Ecuador's tierra caliente contain more than ten thousand species of plants. These flora include ferns, palms, bamboo, and tropical fruits. Many plants are entangled with thick vines, called lianas. Lianas root in the ground and climb up around tree trunks. Such vines can eventually strangle the host plant with their octopuslike tentacles. Epiphytes also thrive in parts of Ecuador. These plants grow on other plants and get moisture and nutrients from the air. They include mosses, lichens, and orchids.

Yasuni National Park in El Oriente boasts some of the most diverse species of plants and animals in the world.

The *toquilla* (also called the *jipijapa*) is a palmlike tree growing in Ecuador's northwestern coastal forests. Vegetable ivory comes from the seeds of the native *tagua* tree. Local craftspeople carve buttons and other ornaments from this natural substance. Giant bamboo trees thrive along the nation's tropical riverbanks, sometimes reaching 60 feet (18 m) in height. Ecuadorians use these massive trees for building houses along the coast. Forests of mangrove trees once thrived along the nation's coast and estuaries (where rivers meet the ocean). However, many of these trees have suffered due to intense shrimp farming in these areas.

Many familiar fruits—such as oranges, lemons, grapefruits, coconuts, apricots, papayas, and pomegranates—grow in Ecuador's warm climate. But more unusual types also flourish. For example, the flesh of the cherimoya fruit tastes like a blend of strawberry, pineapple, and banana flavors. The *naranjilla*, a small yellow fruit, has a distinctive taste midway between a peach and an orange. The *mammee's* hard rind protects a soft, red pulp, and the purple-and-white pepino fruit resembles a cucumber.

Ecuador has an equally broad range of animals. The widest variety of creatures lives in the country's dense rain forests and eastern El Oriente. Jaguars, ocelots, porcupines, and monkeys find homes in the jungle. The peccary—a wild, piglike creature with sharp tusks—feeds on plants and moves about at night. So does the tapir, an odd-looking mammal that resembles a combination of a pig and an elephant. Busy anteaters use their long noses and tongues to poke into anthills and rotten wood. Burrowing armadillos roll up in their hard, scaly shells when frightened. The world's largest rodent—the pig-sized capybara—also makes its home in Ecuador's forests, fleeing to lakes and streams when in danger. At greater altitudes, highland herders watch over flocks of fluffy pack animals such as llamas, vicuñas, and alpacas. Some indigenous people in the southern sierra make rugs and garments from the warm hair of these animals.

Ecuador is the winter home of many North American birds. It also contains many native winged creatures. Bright-feathered parrots, macaws, *cotingas*, and jacamars all flit through Ecuador's forests. Some of the noisiest jungle birds include the horned screamer and trumpeter bird. The white-crested bellbird's startled cry sounds like the clap of a bell. Ecuadorian skies are also filled with hawks, falcons, and vultures. Andean condors, whose image appears on Ecuador's national seal, live in the nation's mountains. In the early 1800s, the German scientist Alexander von Humboldt watched condors circling over Chimborazo's peak, above 23,000 feet (7,010 m). Charles Darwin saw a condor sail in the air for more than half an hour without once flapping its great wings, which are wider than 10 feet (3 m) from tip to tip.

Amphibians such as frogs and toads and reptiles such as the boa constrictor and other snakes also make homes in Ecuador. Sea life including manta rays, sharks, and turtles swim in the nation's coastal waters. Its rivers are home to many fish, as well as mammals including the Amazonian manatee and the Amazonian river dolphin. Another river dweller is the giant otter, which can be up to 6 feet (1.8 m) long. Ecuadorians sometimes call this animal the *lobo del río* (wolf of the river).

Scientists have also long been drawn to the flora and fauna of the Galápagos Islands. A large percentage of the reptiles, fish, and plants living in the waters of this archipelago are found nowhere else on the globe. Seals and penguins swim the Peru Current as it moves northward off Ecuador's coast and reaches the Galápagos. Giant iguanas (a kind of lizard) like those described by Charles Darwin still roam the islands. So do the huge tortoises—some weighing as much as 500 pounds (227 kilograms). But these tortoises are at risk of extinction, as for many years hunters killed them for their meat. Other unusual Galápagos creatures are the short-eared owl and the blue-footed booby. The archipelago's flightless cormorants stand on the beaches, flap their short wings, and croak.

Visit www.vgsbooks.com for links to websites with information about Ecuador's amazing array of plants and animals, from the rain forest in El Oriente to the Galápagos Islands in the Pacific Ocean.

Natural Resources and Environmental Challenges

Ecuador's oil reserves are by far its most economically valuable natural resource. Large petroleum (unrefined oil) deposits east of the Andes have brought great wealth to some Ecuadorians. Other mineral resources include metals such as gold, silver, and copper. Salt, sulfur, and gypsum are also found in Ecuador.

Another important resource is timber. Dense jungles cover about half of Ecuador. The wood of these forests is useful for construction and fuel. In addition, some wooded areas have agricultural potential. Along the coast, forests have been cleared to make room for farms growing coffee, cacao (source of cocoa), and other crops.

But Ecuador's two biggest assets have also brought big problems for the nation's environment. Oil drilling and production has polluted regional waters, including in the Amazon River Basin and

Rain forest land was cleared to make room for the oil industry. Most of Ecuador's petroleum deposits are found in El Oriente. Much of the oil is then transported westward across the Andes to the Pacific coast for export.

the ocean surrounding the Galápagos Islands. Too much logging and clearing of the nation's valuable timber has led to widespread deforestation, or loss of woodlands. Roads built for transporting oil also contributed to this problem, as did shrimp farmers who cut down coastal mangrove trees. Some experts rank Ecuador as the South American nation with the highest rate of deforestation. And deforestation in turn leads to soil erosion and desertification, or the spread of drylands.

The Galápagos Islands, with their unique environment, also face challenges. The growing human population on the islands causes stress for island wildlife and brings new pollution to the area.

The Ecuadorian government has taken some steps to address these issues. Some areas of the nation are officially protected from development, and leaders have vowed to clean up oil pollution. Many species of wildlife—especially in the Galápagos Islands—are also protected. But international agencies have criticized Ecuador for not doing enough to save its diverse environment.

Cities and Towns

Although Ecuador is a small country, contrasts in climate and elevation distinguish the settings of its towns and regions. Coastal cities bear little resemblance to those of the sierra, and El Oriente has a frontier character all its own.

Guayaquil was founded in the 1500s by the Spanish at the site of an indigenous village. A major fire in 1896 destroyed large portions of the city. As a result, few original, historic buildings are left.

GUAYAQUIL (officially called Santiago de Guayaquil) is Ecuador's largest city. It has an estimated population of more than 2.1 million people in the city itself and about 1 million more in the surrounding area. This bustling port is located on the banks of the Guayas River, in humid tropics about 40 miles (64 km) east of the Pacific Ocean. The Guayas is one of Ecuador's busiest waterways. Its traffic includes many kinds of boats, from dugout canoes and balsa rafts to huge freighters and passenger ships. Guayaquil's modern port facilities have helped to make it an important shipping hub that handles most of Ecuador's international trade.

QUITO, Ecuador's capital, is the nation's second-largest city. It is home to about 1.5 million people. The capital perches at an elevation of about 9,300 feet (2,835 m). Few cities have a more beautiful setting than Quito. Quito is also one of the Western Hemisphere's most historic capitals. It was founded by the Spanish in 1534 on the ruins of an Inca city. Quito is famous for its colonial-era art, which is found in more than one hundred churches, chapels, convents, and monasteries.

CUENCA, with a population of more than 300,000, is located 200 miles (322 km) south of Quito. The city is a living museum of Ecuadorian history. More than 450 years ago, the Inca emperor Huayna Capac built the town of Tomebamba on the site. He intended the town to be a rest stop on the mountain road from Cuzco (in southern Peru) to Quito. He also constructed a fortress at nearby Ingapirca. In 1557 Spaniards began to build Cuenca on the foundations of Tomebamba. The cobblestone streets and red-tiled roofs left by the Spanish remind visitors of Cuenca's colonial history.

HISTORY AND GOVERNMENT

For many centuries, the area that later became Ecuador was known as the kingdom of Quito. The region was named after the Quitus people. This indigenous group lived there in pre-Columbian times (before the arrival of Christopher Columbus). Archaeologists believe that many different native peoples once lived in Ecuador. These groups spoke dialects (language variations) of the regional Chibchan language family. Some indigenous peoples in Colombia, Panama, and northwestern Ecuador share similarities in dress, crafts, and speech. These ties have led some historians to suspect that the groups have a common heritage.

 ## Pre-Columbian Era

Most of Ecuador's coastal indigenous peoples were hunters and fishers. They traded their goods with other groups, using dugout canoes and large balsa rafts with sails. They offered salt, fish, parrots, monkeys, and achiote (seeds that yield a dye). They exchanged these goods for

cloth, blankets, and precious metals possessed by the native peoples of the highlands.

With the exception of the Cayapa and the Colorado, these coastal groups either disappeared or intermarried with other groups. Although Ecuador's pre-Columbian peoples spoke different languages, they shared many customs. For example, most highland peoples farmed small plots of land. They grew native crops, such as beans, squash, corn, potatoes, and quinoa (a grain). These mountain farmers also raised some domesticated animals, including guinea pigs for eating. Highland families lived in wood-framed, mud-plastered houses with grass-thatched roofs. Their clothing usually consisted of long, sleeveless shirts or wraparound skirts, with shoulder blankets for warmth.

Because the region's groups were often hostile toward one another, the men were often at war. Consequently, the women did much of the farmwork. When the men were not fighting, they wove textiles, carved tools, and made weapons of metal or stone.

ANCIENT MAIL CARRIERS

Inca leaders made many changes and developments in their empire. One of their projects was building a road that ran the mountainous route from the southern Inca capital of Cuzco to Quito, the main city of the northern provinces. This road was 1,250 miles (2,012 km) long. Relay runners called *chasquis* carried messages from one part of the Inca Empire to another. The messages they carried kept the empire's officials in contact.

◯ Under the Inca Empire

The Inca Empire was a huge and powerful South American realm based in Peru. In the 1400s, it took control of Ecuador's region. But even under Inca influence, Ecuador's indigenous peoples held onto their cultural identities. For example, powerful chieftains continued to rule small estates and to have many wives. Other customs were similar to those of the Incas. Members of the highest social class, for instance, wore fancy clothes and jewels that showed their high rank.

Ecuador's peoples were among the last groups the Incas subdued. The Inca Empire never completely absorbed these local peoples. The Incas had to make compromises to control Ecuadorian peoples. For example, Inca rulers allowed conquered Ecuadorian chieftains to keep many of their traditional privileges.

Ancient Incas used these stone-lined circular pits as storage areas. To learn more about the **Inca ruins in Ingapirca *(above)*** and about the fascinating Inca culture, visit www.vgsbooks.com.

Inca rule in Ecuador lasted about one hundred years. During that time, the Incas built roads, brought in new crops and animals, and introduced their Quechua language. Inca rulers divided the conquered groups into *ayllus*, clans of people who lived together and shared cropland. The empire's subjects paid taxes to the Lord Inca by working on imperial farms or mines, or on crews that built roads, bridges, forts, and temples.

In about 1525, the Lord Inca Huayna Capac was touring his northern domain. While there, he learned that messengers had sighted two strange ships along the coast. Rumors spread that these strangers represented a powerful civilization. The stories alarmed the Inca ruler, who saw omens of an approaching struggle.

Atahualpa

Soon after the sighting of the ships—which turned out to be Spanish—Huayna Capac died. But he had not named an heir to his empire. A bloody struggle for control broke out between two of his sons, Atahualpa and Huáscar. Atahualpa, the more popular son, lived in the northern part of the realm. Eventually he defeated and killed Huáscar, his half-brother. Atahualpa became ruler of the entire Inca territory.

Spanish Exploration and Conquest

In 1526 a Spanish explorer named Bartolomé Ruiz arrived in Ecuador from Panama. He had brought one of fellow explorer Francisco Pizarro's ships to explore the lands to the south. Ruiz visited native people near Esmeraldas. He noticed that their leaders wore gold, silver, and emeralds. After collecting samples, he returned to Panama and reported his findings.

Pizarro himself arrived from Panama in 1532. He met with Atahualpa, the new Lord Inca, in Cajamarca (in modern-day Peru). Taking advantage of Inca disunity due to the recent civil war, Pizarro imprisoned the leader. He and his small group of men also had firearms that were superior to Inca spears and other weapons. Offering the Spaniards a ransom for his freedom, Atahualpa suggested that his subjects fill three rooms with gold and silver. Pizarro accepted the offer. The Lord Inca issued the order, and the precious metals began to flow to Cajamarca.

Then, with the ransom in hand, Pizarro had the Lord Inca killed. The Spaniard justified the deed by calling it punishment for Atahualpa's

In 1532 **Atahualpa *(left, holding staff)* met with Spanish troops.** Francisco Pizarro took the Inca leader prisoner and later executed him.

earlier murder of Huáscar. But his claim of justice did not convince the Lord's subjects. When the Incas learned of their emperor's death, warfare broke out between the Incas and the Spaniards. The weakened Inca Empire soon fell apart, however. The Spaniards moved in to take control and began setting up a colonial government.

Spain did not completely conquer the northern territory of the Inca Empire until 1534. In that year, one of Atahualpa's best generals, Rumiñahui, suffered severe losses in a battle near Riobamba. He and his troops withdrew to the city of Quito, and Rumiñahui ordered his men to burn the settlement. Finding the former Inca power in ashes, Sebastián de Belalcázar founded San Francisco de Quito on the site in December 1534.

◉ Colonial Days

In 1539 Francisco Pizarro named his half-brother Gonzalo governor of Quito. Governor Pizarro's appetite for wealth was fed by legends of El Dorado—Spanish for "the golden one." The tales said that this land was rich in gold, as well as cinnamon and other valuable spices. Gonzalo Pizarro organized an expedition from Quito in 1541 to search for these riches in El Oriente's jungles. Pizarro, Francisco de Orellana, and a large group of men traveled eastward across the Andes to the Coca River. There they built light boats to travel deeper into the jungle.

When the group sent Orellana and a small crew ahead to find food, currents swept their boat into the Napo River and on to the Amazon River.

Legends say that, as Orellana and his crew traveled eastward to the Atlantic Ocean, a group of warrior women attacked them. The Spanish sailors called the women "las Amazonas," after legendary Greek women warriors. Although Orellana did not find the fabled land of gold and spices, his discovery of the mighty Amazon River brought him great rewards and acclaim in Spain.

The king of Spain soon took steps to strengthen his colonial government in the New World of the Americas. In 1543 Spain established the Viceroyalty of Peru. This administrative area included Peru, Ecuador, and other Spanish colonies in South America.

Meanwhile, the native peoples of Ecuador endured hardships under the colonists. The Spanish government had officially pledged to protect these indigenous Ecuadorians. In practice, however, Spain often exploited them. Spanish settlers in the colonies forced local residents to work on their farms and in their households as slaves. Wealthy Spaniards bought and sold these people as part of large agricultural estates.

At the same time, the Spanish introduced their religion of Roman Catholicism to their new subjects. In 1545 the Spanish government placed Quito under the control of a Catholic official called a bishop. The Spaniards hoped that this change would help them convert Ecuadorians to Roman Catholic beliefs, and it also served the religious needs of the Spanish colonists. As time went by, some Ecuadorians did adopt the religion, although many blended its practices with those of their traditional faiths.

In 1563 Spain promoted the Quito area to the higher administrative status of an *audiencia*. Under Spanish rule, however, Quito still belonged to the larger Viceroyalty of Peru.

For the next two hundred years, the Audiencia of Quito experienced the mixed advantages of Spanish-imposed peace. The Spaniards introduced wheat farming and brought domesticated animals, such as pigs, sheep, cattle, horses, and donkeys. But at the same time, they continued exploiting local peoples. They also imported black slaves from Africa to labor on sugarcane plantations along the coast, where there were few native workers.

Even as many native people suffered, the Spanish colonists viewed the audiencia as experiencing steady progress. The city of Quito, in

TALL TALES

Francisco de Orellana and his crew were not the only ones to tell stories about mysterious warrior women. Ancient Greek myths described a nation of fierce female fighters. In fact, Orellana—who was the first European explorer of the Amazon River—named the waterway after these Greek legends.

particular, thrived. It became famous as an artistic center. Quito's churches and public buildings were among the finest Spanish colonial architecture in the Americas.

Independence

In the late 1700s, Quito's people began longing for independence from Spain. They resented that Spain gave the highest posts in the audiencia to those of Spanish birth. Creoles in Quito were inspired by successful wars of independence in France and the United States. (Creoles were people of Spanish descent who were born in the colony but excluded from high office.) And they saw their own chance for freedom when French emperor Napoleon Bonaparte invaded Spain in 1808. The weakened nation lost some of its power over its distant South American colonies. In 1809 and 1810, uprisings took place in Quito. Discontented Creoles stirred up many of these revolts. Though early attempts at revolution failed, the desire for independence grew.

In 1821 the armies of Simón Bolívar and José Francisco de San Martín met on the audiencia's territory. Both Bolívar and San Martín had led independence movements in other parts of South America. Both hoped to help liberate Ecuador next. On May 24, 1822, Antonio José de Sucre, Bolívar's most trusted general, won a victory over Spain at the Battle of Pichincha near Quito. This battle marked the official beginning of Ecuador's independence.

This 1899 painting shows a meeting between José Francisco de San Martín and Simón Bolívar in 1821. The two men and their armies joined forces to fight for Ecuador's independence from Spain.

The Early Republic

During Ecuador's first fifteen years as a nation, Juan José Flores dominated its government and politics. Flores was a Venezuelan-born general and a hero of Ecuador's war of independence. He oversaw the adoption of a national constitution and was elected as Ecuador's first president.

Juan José Flores

But Flores represented the interests of conservative *serranos* (highlanders). Most serranos—centered in Quito—were Catholic landowners of large sierra estates. These wealthy Ecuadorians had long influenced the region's politics, and hoped to keep doing so. But Flores soon ran into conflicts with more liberal *costeños* (lowlanders), who were centered in Guayaquil. These people wanted change. They called for greater rights and democracy for all of Ecuador's citizens—regardless of their wealth or religion. In 1845 these conflicts forced Flores from power.

Turbulent years lay ahead for Ecuador. Ongoing tensions between conservative Quito and liberal Guayaquil resulted in frequent civil disturbances. Border conflicts also broke out with Peru and Colombia. Between 1845 and 1860, eleven different presidents and several military juntas (unelected ruling councils) held power in Ecuador. During this period, local leaders were wary of giving up their independence. They prevented the formation of a strong central government.

Out of these unsettled conditions, Gabriel García Moreno rose to power. García Moreno was a conservative leader with strong ties to the Roman Catholic Church. Either directly through the presidency or indirectly through personal influence, García Moreno went on to control Ecuador's fortunes from 1860 to 1875. Using the landowning upper class and the Church as his power base, García Moreno began reorganizing the nation. His agenda included increasing agricultural production, building railroads and highways, developing foreign trade, and stimulating industry. He achieved these advances, however, at the expense of Ecuadorians' personal freedoms. He stifled and punished political disagreement. He also placed all education under the Catholic Church. Giving the Church even greater power, García Moreno oversaw the creation of an 1869 constitution stating that only practicing Catholics could be citizens.

García Moreno also tried to stamp out liberal sentiments—particularly those that clearly separated church and state. Nevertheless, a strong anti-García Moreno movement emerged. The movement

Eugène Damblans depicted the **assassination of García Moreno.** The illustration ran in a French Catholic weekly magazine in 1921.

ended with García Moreno's assassination on the steps of the presidential residence in 1875.

The following twenty years saw continued conflict. Conservative highlanders still tried to maintain control over Ecuadorian politics. But Guayaquil's liberal residents had been enriched by Ecuador's growing international connections, and they continued to gain power. In 1895 General Eloy Alfaro, leader of the Guayaquil liberals, won control of the government in a coup d'état (seizure of power). Later he was elected president under the new constitution of 1897.

Changes and Challenges

Liberalism thrived in Ecuador under Alfaro's administration. It continued under General Leónidas Plaza Gutiérrez, who governed from 1901 to 1905. Church and state were separated, and education was removed from Catholic control. The government passed laws allowing divorce, requiring civil (nonreligious) marriage registration, and guaranteeing freedom of the press and of religion. The state also took control of all Church-owned property that was not used directly for religious purposes. Health care, education, transportation, and public utilities all improved. And in 1908, Ecuadorians celebrated the completion of the Guayaquil-Quito Railway, an impressive but costly feat of engineering.

But a growing rivalry between Alfaro and Plaza Gutiérrez caused disruption. Their struggle for power erupted into violence when a

A painting by José Grijalva shows **workers building the railroad between Guayaquil and Quito.** The project, started in 1872 under García Moreno, was finished in 1908.

mob supporting Plaza Gutiérrez killed Eloy Alfaro in 1912. Upon his return to power, Plaza Gutiérrez continued his earlier progressive administration. He began reforms in education and authorized work on new railway lines. But Plaza Gutiérrez soon realized that Ecuador was heavily in debt. The nation owed most of this debt to the Commercial and Agricultural Bank of Guayaquil. The bank had grown very wealthy by investing in the development of Ecuador's sugar, petroleum, and manufacturing industries. Its bankers soon replaced the Roman Catholic Church as Ecuador's most powerful nongovernmental group.

New challenges struck in the 1930s, with a worldwide depression (severe economic downturn). Ecuador, like countries elsewhere, wrestled with severe economic and social problems. These difficulties led to greater division between liberal and conservative groups. Factions and new parties rallied around various leaders. On the national level, presidents, dictators, and military juntas replaced one another in rapid succession. None was in office long enough to make real progress confronting Ecuador's problems.

Ecuadorian politics remained troubled through the end of the 1930s. Taking advantage of the unsettled situation, Peruvian troops entered Ecuador in 1941. These forces aimed to take control of lands that Peru's leaders claimed belonged to their nation. Peru's soldiers defeated Ecuadorian forces after a month of intense fighting. In 1942 officials of the two nations met in Rio de Janeiro, Brazil, and signed an

A ROCKY START

During Ecuador's first ninety-five years as an independent nation, it had a succession of forty presidents, dictators, and military juntas. From 1925 to 1948, none of the twenty-two chiefs of state completed the term of office decreed by law.

agreement called the Rio Protocol. The agreement ended the border conflict for the time being. But Ecuador lost more than 75,000 square miles (194,249 sq. km) of El Oriente territory to Peru. Recovery of that land would become an ongoing goal for many Ecuadorian leaders.

In 1948 Ecuador's voters elected Galo Plaza Lasso as president. This election brought a period of progressive rule and better economic fortunes for the nation. Plaza Lasso was the son of former president Leónidas Plaza. Plaza Lasso had been educated in the United States. He had then returned to Ecuador with valuable expertise in farming, especially techniques for breeding dairy cattle. Plaza Lasso became the first president since 1924 to complete a four-year presidential term.

Plaza Lasso's democratic administration respected individual freedoms and allowed the free flow of information. As president, he made plans to improve crop farming and livestock raising and to protect the land through soil conservation. His administration urged highlanders to move out of the thickly populated sierra to the lesser populated lowlands. When a disease wiped out banana crops in Central America, Plaza Lasso helped develop banana growing in Ecuador. During Plaza Lasso's term of office, Ecuador became the world's main banana exporter.

◉ Ups and Downs

Plaza's leadership showed signs of progress. But it was not representative of Ecuador's turbulent history. A more typical political figure was José María Velasco Ibarra, who followed Plaza as president. When he was elected in 1952, Ibarra had already been in office several times. Repeatedly elected by urban voters, Velasco Ibarra made rousing speeches that appealed to the poor. But once in office, he seldom satisfied the hopes he raised while running for office. More than once, his time in power ended with his overthrow.

When Velasco Ibarra took office again in 1952, Ecuador was enjoying economic growth. Velasco Ibarra began a successful term by following the Plaza administration's practices. Railway- and road-building programs went forward, Ecuador's foreign trade increased, and the government was able to balance its financial books. Prevented by the constitution from immediate reelection, Velasco Ibarra completed his term and handed power over to Camilo Ponce Enríquez.

Ponce Enríquez became the third president in a row to take office peacefully and constitutionally.

Velasco Ibarra spent most of the next four years living abroad. He returned in 1960 to win election to a fourth term as president by a large majority of votes. But his views often clashed with those of the military and its officers. A worsening economic situation soon forced Velasco Ibarra to resign. An extended period of military rule followed.

This military period ended in 1968 with the election of Velasco Ibarra to a fifth and final presidential term. He faced a steadily declining economy, widespread public protest, and student riots. In response to these issues, Velasco Ibarra suspended the constitution and dissolved the congress in 1970. At first, Ecuador's military leadership supported these drastic actions. But by 1972, Velasco Ibarra's policies had enraged the military so much that—for the fourth time—a military junta forced him from office. A series of military regimes followed once again.

Beginning in 1934, José María Velasco Ibarra served as president five times and was thrown out of office by Ecuador's military four times.

Meanwhile, big changes were taking place in Ecuador. Oil had been discovered in El Oriente just a few years earlier, in 1967. Oil began to flow in the 1970s—the same period when world oil prices reached a new peak. Oil brought Ecuador a staggering $270 million per month.

Not all Ecuadorians shared equally in the oil profits, however. Those who participated in oil-related activities were able to make fortunes. These lucky few included government officials—whose approval kept the oil flowing—and workers involved in actual oil production, such as manual laborers. Lawyers, accountants, and businesspeople also got into the oil business. Even officers of the armed forces got involved by organizing troops to protect the oil from real or imagined threats.

A civilian government finally returned to Ecuador with new elections in 1979. But in the 1980s, falling international oil prices brought a sharp drop in Ecuador's earnings. By 1986 oil prices were less than half what they had been in 1979. Throughout the rest of the decade, Ecuadorian leaders struggled to cope with their suddenly weak economy. They also faced social turmoil that came with the decline. Trying to improve the country's fortunes, the government cut spending. As a result, programs to develop natural resources and to build new roads lost funding. At the same time, inflation (rapidly rising prices) lowered the value of Ecuadorian workers' paychecks.

Sixto Durán Ballén became Ecuador's president in 1992. He began a campaign of privatization, in which state-owned companies were

THE COST OF OIL

Oil remains one of Ecuador's most important products and exports. But oil wealth does not come without a price. For example, in 2001 an oil tanker spilled more than 200,000 gallons (757,082 liters) of fuel near the Galápagos Islands. As the oil slick seeped toward the islands' precious habitat, Ecuadorian officials declared a state of emergency. They called for international help in cleaning up the spill. But the disaster took a heavy toll on Galápagos wildlife, especially marine iguanas.

Other oil-related worries arose in February 2002 when protests erupted against a new oil pipeline's path. The pipeline cut through a bird sanctuary. It also passed through land with high volcanic activity. As a result, the risk of the pipeline rupturing and spilling oil into these unique and valuable environments is very high.

Indigenous groups have also protested against the oil industry. They argue that petroleum production in Ecuador places native peoples at greater risk and disrupts their lives more than those of wealthier Ecuadorians in the Costa. For example, drilling takes place in the traditional homeland of El Oriente groups. In addition, the nation's pipelines run through the highland homes of other native communities.

sold to foreign investors. By selling Ecuador's state-owned companies, Durán Ballén planned to raise cash needed to pay the nation's debts. Many state-employed workers opposed this plan because they feared the loss of their jobs. Nevertheless, privatization began.

◉ Ongoing Issues

In the second half of the 1990s, corruption and other problems became more prominent than economic issues. In January 1995, an old conflict flared up when Ecuadorian and Peruvian soldiers clashed several times along the border. Agreements signed later that year and in 1996 opened the border region, for the first time in many years, to commercial and civilian traffic.

New political troubles followed. In 1997 the legislature removed President Abdalá Bucaram for corruption, following several days of public protests against him. The congress chairperson, Fabián Alarcón, became president until a national presidential election was held in 1998. Jamil Mahaud, a former mayor of Quito, became the new president. That same year, the government prepared and approved a new constitution. This document made reforms to the nation's court system, restricted some powers of Congress, and strengthened the executive branch.

Later in 1998, Mahaud helped negotiate a new peace treaty with Peru that addressed the border and territory dispute. But the president did not successfully handle the nation's larger economic and social problems. Matters worsened in 1999, when two of the nation's industries had a terrible year. Bad weather ruined harvests from Ecuador's farms, and falling oil prices damaged the economy. Even when oil prices began turning around, new problems arose. Taxi drivers and other transportation workers organized huge strikes (work stoppages) to protest high fuel costs within Ecuador. Meanwhile, inflation had rocketed to more than 90 percent. The nation soon could not pay its international loans. Ecuador had to turn to the International Monetary Fund (IMF) for help managing its debts.

Mahaud's popularity steadily fell. It hit rock bottom in January 2000, when he eliminated the national currency, the sucre, and replaced it with the U.S. dollar. This practice of dollarization was not new in South America. Other financially troubled nations had begun using the stronger dollar in an effort to boost their economies. But the measure was hugely unpopular in Ecuador. It widened the gap between poor citizens—who found it hard to turn in their sucres for dollars—and rich citizens, many of whom already had invested in dollars.

Ecuador's former sucre currency was named after Antonio José de Sucre, the general who led the important battle of independence in May 1822.

Despite the fact that dollarization began lowering inflation, increased unrest soon followed the move. Major anti-Mahaud demonstrations broke out in Quito that same month. The protests ended in Mahaud's overthrow, and once again a military junta took charge of the nation. Shortly afterward, Mahaud's vice president, Gustavo Noboa Bejerano, took charge as the new president. Noboa continued to work to improve Ecuador's financial situation. But he had made little progress by 2002, when Lucio Gutiérrez was elected as his successor.

Gutiérrez was a former military officer who had taken part in Mahaud's 2000 ousting. Like the attempts of many presidents before him, Gutiérrez's efforts to prop up the nation's economy failed. Continued inflation made even basic goods very expensive for Ecuador's people. In addition, corruption accusations plagued Gutiérrez's government. Discontent rose around the country, erupting in 2005 with protests in Quito.

Gutiérrez responded by declaring a state of emergency in April 2005. The declaration brought nightly curfews, bans on protests, and military patrols. Gutiérrez also dismissed the Supreme Court, claiming that its judges were biased against him and his administration.

Critics condemned these drastic moves. They compared them to the actions of a dictator, or a leader with total power. Still more demonstrations followed, and Congress held a special session to discuss the situation. Within a few days, Congress had removed Gutiérrez from office and made his vice president, Alfredo Palacio González, president.

Palacio was in office for only about a year and a half. But he also faced demonstrations. In 2006 indigenous groups protested foreign control of the oil industry. And Palacio, too, declared a state of emergency in response.

In 2007 Rafael Vicente Correa Delgado became president. During his campaign, he had made many bold promises and calls for change. He pledged to stamp out corruption. Many of his plans targeted the nation's ongoing financial woes, as well as social issues. For example, he proposed reforms to the nation's oil industry to benefit poor Ecuadorians. He also opposed forming new and closer economic ties with the United States—ties that he said helped North Americans more than Ecuadorians.

Ecuador's voters liked what they heard. Beginning his presidential term in January 2007, Correa turned to enacting his promises. He began addressing the nation's heavy international debts by asking the IMF and the World Bank (another international financial institution) to renegotiate the amounts and interest. He also called for voters to elect an assembly to review and amend the 1998 constitution. The assembly began meeting in November 2007. Its members soon voted to dissolve the nation's congress, claiming it was riddled with corruption.

Rafael Correa speaks the Quechua language that many indigenous Ecuadorians use. This connection to indigenous voters—who have often distrusted mainstream politicians—won him widespread support among native peoples during his presidential campaign.

But congress members resisted the vote, even when crowds of Correa followers stormed the congress building in support of the move. And Correa soon faced another challenge. In March 2008, Colombian forces launched a raid across the border into Ecuador. The troops targeted and killed several members of a rebel group called the Revolutionary Armed Forces of Colombia (FARC). The event quickly sparked international friction. Colombian leaders said their actions were justified as part of the fight against terrorism. But Ecuadorian officials stated that Colombia had violated Ecuador's rights, and Correa called the attack a "massacre." Venezuela also condemned Colombia's actions. Ecuador and Venezuela stationed troops along the Colombia-Ecuador border, and the threat of war arose. Peace negotiations among the nations soon took place in the Dominican Republic and resulted in a settlement, but tensions remained high.

Government

Ecuador's 1998 constitution provides for a republican form of government, with a chief executive, a legislature, and a supreme court. Voting is compulsory for every Ecuadorian citizen who can read and write and who is between eighteen and sixty-five years of age. The adult illiterate population may also vote, but is not required to do so.

Voters directly elect the president to a four-year term. The president, who may not serve multiple terms in a row, appoints a cabinet (presidential advisers) and other administrative employees.

The 1998 constitution decrees that Ecuador's voters elect the nation's congress. These voters choose from a candidate list compiled by national political parties. Voters elect national congresspeople as well as representatives for each of the country's twenty-two provinces. The congress comprises several smaller committees, each of which focuses on a specific subject. Legislators pass laws, address budget issues, and ratify international treaties.

Ecuador's highest court is the Supreme Court, made up of thirty justices. The congress chooses the court's justices, who are appointed for life. The judicial system also includes a Constitutional Court, which reviews laws and cases based on their constitutionality. Judges on this court serve for four years. Lower levels of the judicial system include regional courts and courts for appealing previous sentences.

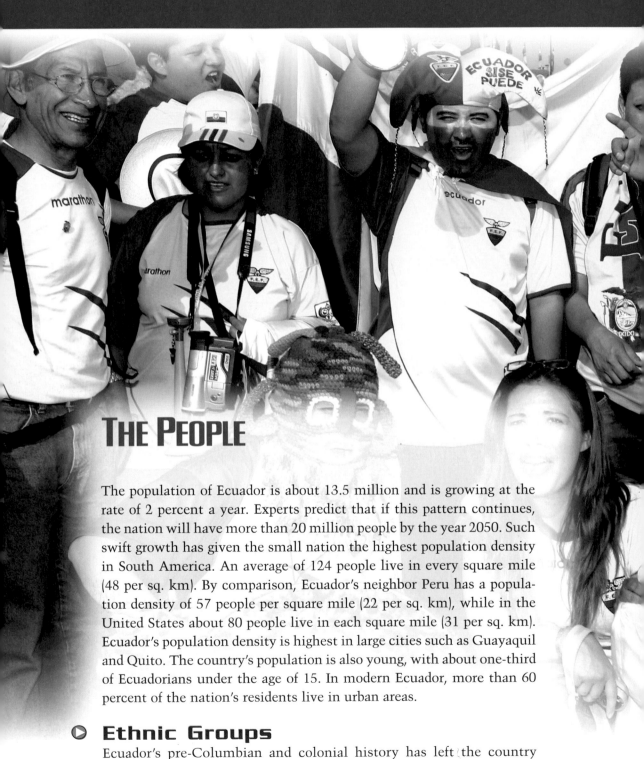

THE PEOPLE

The population of Ecuador is about 13.5 million and is growing at the rate of 2 percent a year. Experts predict that if this pattern continues, the nation will have more than 20 million people by the year 2050. Such swift growth has given the small nation the highest population density in South America. An average of 124 people live in every square mile (48 per sq. km). By comparison, Ecuador's neighbor Peru has a population density of 57 people per square mile (22 per sq. km), while in the United States about 80 people live in each square mile (31 per sq. km). Ecuador's population density is highest in large cities such as Guayaquil and Quito. The country's population is also young, with about one-third of Ecuadorians under the age of 15. In modern Ecuador, more than 60 percent of the nation's residents live in urban areas.

⊙ Ethnic Groups

Ecuador's pre-Columbian and colonial history has left the country with an ethnically varied population. Mestizos—people of mixed

indigenous and European bloodlines—are the largest single group. Estimates of the nation's ethnic breakdown state that mestizos make up about 55 to 65 percent of the nation's people. Another 25 percent or so of citizens are of only indigenous ethnicity. Approximately 7 to 10 percent of Ecuador's population is of only European origin (mostly Spanish). Blacks, who live mainly along the coast, make about another 5 to 10 percent. A very small number of the nation's residents are immigrants from Asia.

Of the once-numerous indigenous peoples of the Costa, few groups remain. Only the Colorado and the Cayapa have kept separate cultural identities. Both of these groups are related to Colombia's Chibcha. However, they speak different languages and have different traditions from one another. Most Colorado and Cayapa are farmers.

In El Oriente, major indigenous groups include the Yumbo, Jivaro, and Auca. The Yumbo are members of a Quechua-speaking people. They live along the banks of the many rivers that flow through El

ECUADOR'S REDHEADS

Santo Domingo de los Colorados is a small town located about 80 mountainous miles (129 km) west of Quito. Santo Domingo has long been known as the home of the indigenous Tsáchila people. In the Spanish language, the Tsáchila are known as the Colorados—Spanish for "red colored." This name comes from the fact that the group's males traditionally rub dye from achiote seeds into their hair to give it a distinctive, reddish color (below).

Oriente. The group is a mixture of many peoples whose individual groups had lost their unity after the Spanish arrived. By adopting one language and by remaining isolated, the Yumbo were able to forge a new identity from different elements.

The Jivaro live in provinces near the Peruvian border. They were once renowned as headhunters (people who collected the heads of their defeated foes as trophies). Modern Jivaro have largely rejected contact with nonindigenous groups. They speak their own language, called Jivaroan or Shuar, but many also know Quechua. Along with the smaller Auca tribe, the Jivaro represent peoples who have preserved their culture, religious beliefs, traditions, and language since pre-Columbian times.

The Otavalo people live northeast of Quito. They have probably had more contact with European influences than any other Ecuadorian native group. They are famous for the excellence of their handwoven textiles, which they market nationwide and beyond. Despite having widespread contact with nonindigenous groups, the Otavalo have maintained a strong cultural identity and set of traditions.

An Otavalo family sells handmade rugs and hats at an outdoor market.

Ecuador's small population of black people has largely remained on the Ecuadorian coast, where its ancestors first arrived. Slaves were once brought here to work on the coastal sugar plantations. In modern Ecuador, most blacks are farmers. Others work as laborers on fishing or cargo boats.

Language

The official language of Ecuador is Spanish. This tongue was brought to the region by Spanish conquerors and colonists. Government offices, schools, and other public institutions use Spanish.

QUECHUA CONVERSATION

Learn a few words and phrases in Ecuador's Quechua language, which comes down from the Incas:

hello:	*napaykullayki*
good-bye:	*ratukama*
please:	*allichu*
thank you:	*yusulipayki*
snowy mountain:	*riti-orko*
river:	*mayu*

But many people also speak indigenous languages. In parts of the highlands and other rural areas, residents often use these native tongues more than they use Spanish. More than ten different indigenous languages exist, but the most commonly spoken are Quechua, Jivaroan, and Chachi. Different indigenous groups often speak dialects of these languages, especially in remote areas.

A teacher in a rural village gives a language lesson in Quechua, a common indigenous language spoken in Ecuador.

Education

Ecuador's public education system was once badly in need of improvement. As the nation's population grew, its schools could not keep up with the number of students. Literacy levels (the number of adults who can read and write) were low. Many children did not attend school at all.

Reforms to Ecuador's public education system over the years have made great strides in providing schooling. Nevertheless, Ecuador still finds it difficult to provide high-quality schooling to all of its people, especially in remote areas.

All Ecuadorian children are required by law to attend school for a total of six years. They must complete these years of schooling sometime when they are between the ages 6 and 14. In modern Ecuador, an average of about 90 percent of the nation's children attend classes. But this figure is higher in cities than it is in rural areas.

Beginning in 1944, the Ecuadorian government began a huge campaign to combat illiteracy. The campaign proved effective over the years, and about 92 percent of modern Ecuador's adults can read and write. Many of them learned basic skills through educational television.

Two of the nation's main institutions of higher learning are the Central University of Ecuador and the Pontifical Catholic University, both located in Quito. The University of Cuenca and the University of Guayaquil are also prominent schools.

Indigenous students in a rural mountain town learn the alphabet.
Ecuador has worked to make sure all children have access to education. Visit www.vgsbooks.com for links to more information about Ecuador's educational system.

Health

Like educational standards, health standards in Ecuador have improved significantly over time. In the 1980s and 1990s, a range of international and national groups tried to improve health care in Ecuador. For instance, the World Health Organization helped vaccinate against diseases in Ecuador. The United Nations Children's Fund contributed money to build a large milk pasteurization plant in Quito, under the condition that part of the milk would be given away free.

In part because of such programs, the average life expectancy of modern Ecuadorians is 75 years of age. This lifespan is 3 years longer than the South American average. The infant mortality rate is 25 deaths out of every 1,000 births. The figure is close to the South American average ratio of 24 per 1,000. It also marks a great improvement, down from 40 out of 1,000 in about 1998. In addition, the rate of HIV/AIDS (human immunodeficiency virus/acquired immunodeficiency syndrome) infection is quite low, affecting 0.3 percent of the population between the ages of 15 and 49.

Challenges remain, however. Typhus, typhoid fever, malaria, yellow fever, and tuberculosis (a lung disease) are contagious diseases that continue to spread in Ecuador. Malnourishment and undernourishment from a lack of enough healthy foods are also problems. In particular, the diet of many poor Ecuadorians lacks proteins and minerals. Foods such as eggs, milk, and fresh vegetables are often too expensive for poor families to buy. One indication of this nutritional issue is that 6 percent of Ecuadorian children less than five years of age are underweight. This figure is in contrast to an average of 4 percent in all of South America and 1 percent in North America.

Many of the country's health issues are more serious among rural populations than they are in urban areas. For instance, it is generally easy to find good clinics and doctors in the country's large cities. On the other hand, many Ecuadorians in the highlands and El Oriente still lack adequate medical attention and hospital facilities.

Similarly, an important factor in preventing disease is access to clean drinking water, as well as good sewer and sanitation facilities. But Ecuadorians living outside cities have much worse water and sanitation systems than those in urban Ecuador. Studies report that only about 89 percent of rural residents have access to improved drinking water, compared to 97 percent in cities. "Improved" drinking water comes from safe sources such as household taps or clean wells. The gap in good sanitation is similar. Just 82 percent of rural Ecuadorians are able to access adequate sanitation facilities, in contrast with 94 percent of urban residents.

Daily Life

Daily life in Ecuador varies around the country. Like other aspects of the nation's character, these variations split mainly along rural and urban lines. Ethnic differences also account for variations in daily habits and general ways of life. But often these two primary factors combine.

For example, mestizos, blacks, and other ethnic groups who live in the cities take part in a highly Spanish-influenced society. That is, they typically live in apartment buildings or other modern housing, with conveniences such as running water and electricity. They commonly work in industrial or office jobs. Many urban Ecuadorians speak only Spanish and do not know indigenous languages.

People living in rural areas, however, frequently follow longstanding indigenous patterns of living. Many homes are one-room dwellings with tiled or thatched roofs. They often lack electricity or running water. Rural residents often do traditional work, such as farming or craftmaking. In addition to Spanish, many speak Quechua or other native languages.

Clothing also differs between the cities and the countryside. City dwellers tend to dress in modern garments such as suits, dresses, and blue jeans. Campesinos (a general name for rural Ecuadorians of all ethnicities) may also adopt some of these styles. But in the highlands and other rural areas, traditional garb is also common. Typical clothing includes woven ponchos (squarish, usually woolen shoulder capes, with a hole in the middle for the wearer's head), flowing short pants, and embroidered blouses.

A family of campesinos stands outside their home in Cañar, east of Guayaquil.

A mother and her children wear traditional clothing while herding llamas in the Andes.

Social Issues and Change

Ecuador has long faced issues of inequality among its people. Women, for example, often face discrimination when they seek jobs. Once in the workplace, women often receive lower pay than their male coworkers, and they may encounter sexual harassment. In addition, many married women suffer physical abuse from their husbands.

Members of the nation's indigenous groups have also experienced discrimination. Ecuador's ethnic mixture has often caused social tensions and unrest. The small minority of Ecuadorians of completely Spanish descent has long had the biggest influence on the nation's economic, political, and social life. Most politicians, wealthy businesspeople, and people who own large tracts of land come from this group. Friction between the elite minority and the larger sections of society has brought about political upheavals and social unrest.

Having been largely ignored by the government for years, native peoples have increasingly demanded to be recognized at the national level. In the early 1990s, indigenous peoples called for the redistribution of large farms. In 1992 the government responded by giving native Ecuadorian groups a large tract of land in El Oriente.

Some politicians have also responded to the call for land reform and other solutions to inequality. While campaigning for the presidency in 2006 and 2007, Rafael Correa pledged to address these issues. He promised to fight for greater rights and governmental representation for all. Indigenous peoples and women around the country are hopeful that he will follow through on these promises.

CULTURAL LIFE

Ecuador's culture is a blend of many backgrounds. The nation's colonial history brought Spanish trends and influence to the region, but they did not erase longstanding indigenous customs. The Roman Catholic religion brought different traditions but never completely took the place of local faiths. And modern times and political troubles have spurred new artistic developments, without overshadowing old crafts and pastimes. This layering of new and old has left Ecuador with a rich and vibrant cultural life.

 Religion

Indigenous peoples in Ecuador have followed a variety of belief systems for centuries. Nature holds an important place in these faiths, which include numerous spirits. Many of the spirits represent aspects of the environment and natural world, such as animals and the weather. Religious figures called shamans act as spokespeople between the people and their deities (gods and goddesses). In El Oriente, the jungle is

central to local beliefs and legends. Coastal groups, on the other hand, revere the sea, fish, snakes, pumas, and jaguars. They have traditionally built richly decorated totem poles to honor those deities. Coastal artisans usually carve these totems with alternating male and female figures, arranged in order from childhood to maturity. Some of the largest totem poles stand 40 feet (12 m) tall.

When Spanish explorers and conquerors reached Ecuador in the 1500s, they brought their Roman Catholic religion. The faith soon became the dominant religion in Ecuador, and it has remained so ever since. The Catholic Church has also frequently played a role in Ecuadorian politics. But in modern Ecuador, the government no longer gives financial support to the Catholic Church or endorses it as an official religion. Ecuador's constitution grants all citizens the freedom to follow any religion they wish, or no religion.

Nevertheless, Roman Catholicism remains by far the nation's dominant religion. An estimated 85 to 87 percent of Ecuadorians consider themselves to be Catholic. But this figure represents a wide range of actual practices. Some Ecuadorians observe the religion strictly and in keeping with standard Catholic traditions. Others, however, attend church rarely and may modify their worship. For example, many indigenous people who have been baptized as Catholics combine parts of the religion with elements of their indigenous faiths. For example, native groups in the highlands tend to merge and blend Catholic saints (holy people) with spirits and deities of local religions. Similarly, many indigenous peoples in El Oriente's jungle regions continue to practice shamanism, sometimes in combination with Catholic rites.

Ecuador also has a small number of Protestants (non-Catholic Christians). The number of Protestants is growing, but the group still makes up only about 10 percent of the population. The remaining percentage of Ecuadorians follow Judaism, Bahai, Islam, and other non-Christian faiths, or are not religious at all.

Holidays and Festivals

Most Ecuadorians are very fond of traditions. Ecuadorians of various religions have preserved many ceremonial rites over the years. They have preserved so many, in fact, that Ecuador's residents celebrate festivals during every month of the year. Some of these occasions are rooted in Catholicism or other faiths, but others are secular (nonreligious).

The year's revelry begins with a bang on Año Viejo—New Year's Eve. To ring in the fresh year, people stuff dolls with rags, fireworks, and eucalyptus tree branches. Many of these figures are humorous representations of political leaders. At midnight, the dolls go up in flames. Among the crowd, some revelers are disguised as black-clad widows who beg for money to pay fiesta expenses.

February brings celebration to the highland town of Ambato, located in central Ecuador. Ambato is home to the Fiesta de las Flores y de las Frutas (Festival of Flowers and Fruits). The two-week event combines secular fun with Christian celebration, as it falls during Carnival, the holiday right before Lent (a somber period leading up to Easter). Ambato residents and hundreds of visitors go all out during the festival, celebrating with bullfights, soccer games, parades, beauty pageants, dancing in the parks, and art exhibits.

Beauty pageants are very popular in Ecuador. Local girls and women participate in these contests during most festivals and special occasions.

On the Christian calendar, the most important holiday of the year is Easter. During Holy Week (the week ending on Easter Sunday), Ecuadorian Christians attend church

A costumed dancer participates in a festival in Latacunga. The festival seeks protection against volcanic eruptions from the nearby Cotopaxi volcano.

services, watch religious processions, and enjoy special holiday meals.

Two major national holidays fall in May. The first day of the month is Labor Day, marked with many parades. Parades fill the streets once again near the end of the month, on May 24. This date marks the anniversary of the Battle of Pichincha and commemorates Ecuador's independence as a nation.

Many harvest festivals take place in September. One is Otavalo's Fiesta del Yamor. This festival celebrates the staple crop of corn, which also symbolizes fertility and generosity. At the same time, it pays honor to Otavalo's patron saint. Festivities include traditional dancing, bullfights, and chilly swimming competitions in the mountain town's San Pablo Lake.

Quito holds a fair in the first week of December that celebrates the capital city's founding. The fair has become a showcase for homemade Ecuadorian goods, and donkey caravans loaded with handicrafts pour in from every province. The days and nights are filled with dances, contests, parties, bullfights, and parades.

In addition to these regional and national holidays, many special occasions center around family life. Events such as baptisms and weddings bring people together in celebration. Another celebration is the *quinceañera*, a girl's fifteenth birthday. This rite of passage marks the girl's entrance into adulthood.

◉ Food

A popular category of foods among Ecuadorian diners is soups and stews. For example, *fanesca* is a stew made from onions, peanuts, fish, rice, squash, beans, corn, and lentils. Many people consider fanesca Ecuador's national dish. It is also a must-have meal on Easter and throughout Holy Week. *Locro* is a stew made from cheese and potatoes, and *seco de chivo* (goat stew) is served with hot rice. Many Ecuadorians also favor fried dishes such as *llapingachos*, fried pancakes made of cheese and potatoes and usually topped with egg or avocado. *Patacones* are plantains (a kind of banana) that have been fried, mashed, and fried again. A zesty accompaniment to many dishes is *ají*, a spicy sauce of hot red peppers, tomatoes, and onions. Diners often pour ají over chicken, plain rice, or almost anything else they like. For those eating on the run, small stands along Ecuadorian roadsides sell *humitas* (sweet-corn cakes with onion, eggs, and spices), empanadas (savory meat-filled pastries), and *choclos* (toasted ears of corn). Ecuadorian beverages include fruit juices, strong coffee, and *chicha*, a drink from Inca times. Usually made from corn, it is a fermented alcoholic beverage.

LLAPINGACHOS

These simple and savory potato-cheese cakes are a popular dish in Ecuador. They can be served as part of a meal or as a hearty snack.

1 pound potatoes, peeled and cut into chunks

¼ teaspoon salt

1 tablespoon butter

1 medium white onion, diced

½ cup shredded white cheese such as Monterey jack or muenster

¼ cup vegetable oil or butter

1. Place the potatoes in a large pot and cover with water. Add ¼ teaspoon of salt and bring to a boil over high heat. Boil for 25 minutes, or until it is easy to pierce the potatoes with a fork. Remove potatoes from heat. Drain the water, and mash potatoes well.
2. Heat butter in a small saucepan over medium heat. Add the onions and sauté for about 5 minutes until soft but not too brown. Remove onions from heat.
3. Mix together the potatoes and onions. Shape the mixture into about twelve balls. Poke a hole in a ball and fill the hole with cheese. Seal the hole and flatten the ball into a patty about ½-inch thick. Repeat with remaining potato-onion balls.
4. Place patties in the refrigerator for about fifteen minutes.
5. Heat oil or butter in a large, heavy saucepan over medium-high heat. Carefully place a few patties in the pan and sauté for about 3 to 5 minutes on each side, or until golden brown. Remove and drain on paper towels. Repeat with remaining patties. Serve warm.

Serves 4 to 6

Seafood stew is featured on many menus in Ecuador.

In coastal areas and along Ecuador's rivers, seafood features in many dishes. Ceviche, fish marinated in lemon or lime juice, is a popular appetizer. Shrimp and catfish are also common. Many cooks use *agua de coco* (coconut water) in seafood dishes. Meat is more common in the highlands. One favorite dish is *churrasco*. It is a hearty combination of meat (usually beef), vegetables, potatoes, rice, eggs, and sometimes avocado.

Indigenous cooks have their own specialties. Native peoples in Ecuador have long preserved meat from alpacas and other animals by salting and drying it. They called the dried meat *charqui*, which has been adopted by English speakers as *jerky* (such as beef jerky). Another traditional ingredient that still sometimes appears in indigenous kitchens is *cuy*—roasted guinea pig. Grains such as corn and quinoa often feature in indigenous dishes.

Literature

In pre-Columbian Ecuador, most indigenous peoples did not have written literary works. Instead, an oral tradition of storytelling connected families, ethnic groups, and communities. Africans in Ecuador also kept their history and traditions alive through telling stories and singing songs.

Ecuadorian literature of the colonial period is often flowery in style. But later work brought in a simpler, nationalistic spirit. José Joaquín de Olmedo was a very important

THREE JUANS ARE BETTER THAN ONE

Ambato's nickname is La Tierra de los Tres Juanes, or "The Land of the Three Juans." It gets this nickname because it is the birthplace of writers Juan María Montalvo Fiallos, Juan Benigno Vela, and Juan León Mera Martínez.

THE LITERARY GALÁPAGOS

The Galápagos Islands feature in many works of fiction and fact. Sailor Alexander Selkirk visited the islands in 1709 after being rescued by British pirates off the coast of Chile. Selkirk was the real-life model for the fictional Robinson Crusoe. In Herman Melville's book *Las Encantadas*, the American writer described his 1841 visit to the Galápagos on a whaling ship. In 1859 Charles Darwin published his account of visiting the Galápagos (in 1835) in *The Voyage of the Beagle*. He called the islands a "living laboratory of evolution." After Charles William Beebe published *Galápagos, World's End* in 1923, people intrigued by his account began moving to live on the islands.

JUAN MONTALVO
ESSAYISTE ET POLEMISTE
1832-1889

Ecuadorian poet. He played an active role in Ecuador's struggle for independence and also served briefly as president. Writer Juan María Montalvo Fiallos is best remembered for his political essays that attacked Gabriel García Moreno (a prominent leader between 1860 and 1875). The classic Ecuadorian novel *Cumandá*, by Juan León Merá Martínez, is set in an indigenous village at the time of independence. It has a native girl as its main character.

In the late 1800s and early 1900s, an artistic movement known as *indigenismo* emerged in South America. This continent-wide style emphasized pride in indigenous pre-Columbian cultures and criticized exploitation of native populations. Many Ecuadorian writers—especially those of the sierra—participated in this movement. Jorge Icaza's novel *Huasipungo* is Ecuador's most famous indigenismo literary work. The story focuses on an indigenous man who labors tirelessly on a small piece of land belonging to a large estate. Icaza's work elevated native peoples to a national symbol of simple virtues and strong faith. But while Icaza's book was popular and important for its time, indigenismo work can also give false

Writer **Juan María Montalvo Fiallos** *(left)* was exiled to Colombia when he published a pamphlet series called *El Cosmopolita* (The Cosmopolitan), some of which viciously attacked Gabriel García Moreno.

impressions. Few of the movement's artists were indigenous people themselves, and their writings sometimes portray native peoples as helpless or primitive.

The poet Jorge Carrera Andrade began publishing work in the 1940s. Carrera Andrade incorporated some indigenismo qualities into his writing. Many of his poems paint vivid images of life in small villages and among native groups. Gonzalo Escudero was writing about the same time, and he used similar themes. Rather than sticking strictly to traditional poetic forms, Carrera Andrade and Escudero focused on simple descriptions of nature that glorified Ecuador's beauty.

More recent authors include the poet Marcelo Báez Meza, whose work focuses on city life and urban experiences in Ecuador. Poet Augusto Rodríguez is an up-an-coming young author who has published several books and won international prizes for his writing. Black authors also bring different perspectives to Ecuadorian literature. For example, Adalberto Ortiz and Nelson Estupiñán Bass both composed poetry and novels describing the poverty and discrimination facing many Ecuadorian blacks. Antonio Preciado Bedoya is a black poet who has also served as Ecuador's Minister of Culture.

◉ Visual Arts

In pre-Columbian times, most art in Ecuador was pottery or ceramic sculpture. Some of these works were connected to ancient religions. With the arrival of the Spaniards, Catholicism took over as a major artistic theme. Painters and sculptors created images of Catholic saints and scenes. Quito has been a particularly important art center since colonial times, and its religious art is famous all over the world. A fusion of native and Spanish culture—called the Quito school—emerged in the capital. It reached its full splendor during the late 1600s and early 1700s. During this period, local artists moved beyond making copies of European art and began developing their own styles. Some images from this group of artists displayed cultural combinations, such as Jesus wearing traditional indigenous clothing. Other works set Christian themes in uniquely Ecuadorian landscapes.

Following Ecuador's independence, the nation's visual artists—like its authors—took part in South America's indigenismo movement. Some of the greatest indigenismo works were murals, or large wall paintings, by Mexican artists. These works in turn inspired Ecuadorian painters. Oswaldo Guayasamín Calero stands out as Ecuador's most important indigenismo artist. Guayasamín Calero's works depict native peoples, mestizos, and blacks in scenes of everyday life. Other muralists include Camilo Egas and Eduardo Kingman.

They used strong, rich colors and simple designs, especially in illustrations of Andean peoples.

More recent styles have focused on reawakening national Ecuadorian identity. Contemporary painter Enrique Tábara combines modern and European-inspired styles with pre-Columbian themes such as shamanism, spirits, and Ecuador's natural world.

In addition to fine arts, Ecuador's people create a wide variety of crafts. Artisans in villages around the country create pottery, gold and silver work, woven products, wood carvings, and leather goods.

Music

Most native Ecuadorian music began as the ritual music of pre-Columbian peoples. The music is based on a five-tone scale (also used in Asia), which often gives it a melancholy sound. While some ancient tunes have been lost, musicians in parts of the highlands still play many of the old songs. Performers play traditional instruments including the *quena* (a clay or bamboo flute) and *rondador* (a panpipe made from a series of bamboo reeds). The people of El Oriente make

Musicians play a song using traditional Ecuadorian instruments, including quenas and a rondador.

percussion instruments out of items such as toucan bird beaks and seed-filled gourds. Traditional highland styles such as *albazo*, *sanjuanito*, and *yumbo* often accompany folk dancing.

The Spanish introduced instruments including the harp, guitar, and violin. South American composers have combined indigenous and Spanish music to produce *música mestiza*. For example, the *yaraví*, an Andean ballad, uses the five-note scale. The *tonada*, a Spanish variation of the same tune, uses a seven-tone scale, which produces a livelier-sounding melody. A style that arose in the 1800s was the very popular *pasillo*. Originating in Ecuador's coastal lowlands but influenced by European themes, pasillo music is slow and sometimes mournful. It has remained a typical and beloved style.

Ecuador opened its national conservatory of music in 1870. The first director, Antonio Neumane, composed music for the country's national anthem. In modern Ecuador, classically trained musicians often blend folk melodies into their compositions. Domenico Brescia included indigenous tunes in his *Ecuadorian Symphony*. Segundo Luis Moreno Andrade, author of a classic book on Ecuadorian music, used native rhythms in his work as well. Local influences are also part of Luis Humberto Salgado Torres's symphonic suite *Atahualpa*.

Modern Ecuadorian bands also create rock, pop, and hip-hop music. Some blend folk music traditions with these newer styles. And many local music lovers enjoy listening to artists from the United States and other nations.

Visit www.vgsbooks.com for links to websites with additional information about the music and culture of Ecuador.

BOMBA BEATS

African influences show clearly in some of Ecuador's music. For example, a mostly black community centered near northern Ecuador's Chota River originated bomba music, which has African roots as well as regional influences. Drumbeats are central to this style.

Sports and Recreation

Ecuadorians are devoted to soccer, call *futbol*—Spanish for "football." Professional and amateur teams play in stadiums throughout the country. In addition, many people organize informal games in

Ecuadorian soccer player **Jimmy Bran** *(right)* of Deportivo Cuenca goes after a ball against Uruguay's Ribair Rodríguez.

villages and towns. Ecuador's national team is nicknamed La Tricolor. It took part in the World Cup—soccer's most important international event—in 2002 and 2006.

Another popular sport is *pelota de guante* (glove ball). The game is played almost exclusively in Ecuador. Participants wear gloves that are attached to round, flat wooden paddles. With these gloves, players hit a heavy rubber ball to each other. Volleyball is another commonly played sport.

Bullfighting came to Ecuador with Spanish colonists. In modern Ecuador, bullfights often coincide with important national festivals, such as Quito's fair in December. Internationally known matadors—mostly from Spain and Mexico—are featured performers.

Other pastimes in Ecuador take advantage of the region's natural beauty. Some locals, as well as many visitors, enjoy outdoor activities such as hiking in the nation's mountains and fishing in its lakes and

Ecuador won its first Olympic gold medal in 1996. Athlete Jefferson Leonardo Pérez Quezada won the award in speed walking.

streams. Beach-going and picnics are also popular activities.

On weekends and evenings, many urban Ecuadorians enjoy going out to nightclubs, discos, and restaurants, especially in Quito and Guayaquil. In smaller towns and villages, social life often centers around the local plaza (town square). People gather in these public spaces to chat and relax.

A Spanish matador performs for a crowd in Quito during the annual bullfight festival.

THE ECONOMY

Ecuador is a small country with a large variety of natural resources. Yet it remains one of South America's most economically underdeveloped nations. This situation exists partly because many people are subsistence farmers who raise only enough food to feed their families. A high birthrate and inadequate transportation facilities have also kept Ecuador's standard of living low. Its annual per capita (person) income is $4,400. That figure is only about half the South American average of $8,790 per person.

Ecuador's sierra and Costa show economic differences. The sierra lacks agricultural land for major farm production and has a surplus of workers. In contrast, the Costa and El Oriente have plenty of land but not a sufficient labor force to develop their resources fully.

Nevertheless, after a long period of decline, Ecuador's economy enjoyed growth in the early 2000s. Outside and unexpected issues can threaten the nation's finances, however. Petroleum, bananas, cacao, and coffee exports are all crucial to the Ecuadorian economy. But these exports are subject to world competition and price fluctuations. As a result, Ecuador's economy often depends on factors beyond the control of the nation or its workers.

Services and Trade

Ecuador's service industry accounts for about 50 percent of the nation's gross domestic product. (Abbreviated as GDP, gross domestic product is a measure of the total annual value of goods and services produced by a nation's workers.) Jobs in the service sector supply services rather than producing goods. Such activities include government work, banking, insurance, health care, retail sales, and tourism. Close to 60 percent of Ecuadorian workers have jobs in the service industry.

Trade is also important to Ecuador's economy. The nation exports products such as petroleum, bananas, cacao, seafood (especially shrimp and canned fish), and flowers. Most of these exports go to the United States, Colombia, Italy, Peru, and Chile.

Workers on a shrimp boat unload their catch at the port in Guayaquil.

Ecuador also imports goods from around the world. The nation purchases items including vehicles, medicines, food products, and raw materials such as iron and steel. Most Ecuadorian imports come from the United States, Colombia, and Japan. Other major sources include Venezuela, Germany, Chile, and Brazil.

Mining and Industry

Together, mining and industry account for about 40 percent of the nation's GDP. They also employ approximately 30 percent of the country's workers.

Petroleum remains Ecuador's major mining industry. In 1972 a pipeline began carrying crude oil across the Andes to the coast for refining and export. Even after the 1980s drop in oil prices, the nation remains one of South America's top oil producers. It is the second largest exporter after Venezuela. Estimates from 2008 stated that the country's oil wells were producing approximately 500,000 barrels a day. In addition, a new pipeline across the Andes began pumping oil in 2003—in spite of protests from environmental groups.

Petroecuador is the nation's state-owned oil company. For many years, the company granted leases to foreign oil companies and collected royalties on petroleum exports. But in 2007 and 2008, finance and oil officials in Ecuador's government began suggesting changes in this system. They proposed that Ecuador's government pay companies a fee to extract the petroleum, after which the petroleum would belong to the state. In addition, after taking office as president in 2007, Rafael

Correa called for a change in handling windfall oil profits. Windfalls are sudden, large profits made due to unpredictable circumstances such as an unexpected rise in prices. Correa called for 99 percent of windfall profits made by foreign oil companies in Ecuador to go to the nation. Former agreements had given 50 percent to Ecuador. Negotiations over such proposals followed, and reforms in the oil industry continue to be a major issue.

While oil is the country's most valuable mining resource, it is not the only one. Ecuadorian workers also mine gold, silver, salt, sulfur, gypsum, copper, lignite (brown coal), and kaolin (clay used in ceramics).

FROM JUNGLE TO OCEAN

Texaco and Gulf oil companies discovered vast petroleum deposits in El Oriente in 1967. But they still needed a way to get the oil out of the jungle—and across the nation's rugged highlands. So the companies constructed the world's highest pipeline. The pipeline climbed up and over the Andes Mountains and down to the hot, humid tropical coast at Esmeraldas, where tankers waited to pick up the oil.

Employees of **Petroecuador, an Ecuadorian oil company,** work to clean up an oil spill in Lago Agrio, a center of oil production in El Oriente.

Ecuador's small domestic market and lack of skilled workers restrict the nation's industrial development. Food processing is the most important part of the manufacturing sector. Other significant industries produce textiles, clothing, shoes, furniture, and fertilizer.

Agriculture and Livestock

Farming comprises a relatively small part of Ecuador's economy. In 2007 agriculture and fishing combined accounted for only about 10 of the nation's GDP. As recently as the 1990s, however, it has made up close to 20 percent. As agricultural production and income fluctuate widely with weather patterns and international prices, experts believe that it may rebound in the future. About 10 percent of the nation's labor force works in agriculture, fishing, forestry, or hunting.

Less than one-quarter of Ecuador's land is farmed. Geographic obstacles and a shortage of cropland in the highlands have hampered development. But to make the most of the nation's farmable land, Ecuadorians have developed specially adapted crops and different land uses for each altitude. Bananas and cacao grow at the lower elevations, coffee and beans thrive in the higher but still temperate regions, and potatoes grow in colder parts of the sierra. Highland farmers often use the region's high plateaus as grazing land for sheep and goats. Major highland crops include beans, corn, wheat, barley, and potatoes. All of these foods are primarily for local consumption rather than export. Pyrethrum—a natural insecticide derived from

A farmer clears fields on the steep slopes of the Andes, using oxen and a hand-driven plow. Most crops in this area are grown for local consumption and for sale at local farmers' markets.

A worker weighs bananas at one of **Ecuador's banana plantations.** Ecuador is the world's largest exporter of bananas.

chrysanthemum flowers—is an important cash crop that Ecuadorians export to foreign countries.

Much of the sierra's land suffers from centuries of constant use as well as from wind and water erosion. Lowland soils are much better, and coastal farming is geared largely to the export market. Valuable cacao, bananas, and coffee all thrive in the lowlands. Other regional crops include sugarcane, rice, yucca (a starchy root), cotton, peanuts, indigo (a plant dye), tobacco, and tropical fruits.

Ecuador is also a leading producer of abaca. Abaca's hard fibers are used in making twine, mats, surgical clothing, disposable diapers, and high-quality paper. Most of the harvest is shipped to the United States—the world's largest importer of abaca.

Livestock raising is another major agricultural pursuit in Ecuador. About two million sheep graze in the highlands, raised mostly for their meat. Herds of dairy cattle also graze Ecuador's highland fields, especially in the plateau that extends from Ibarra to Riobamba. Farmers also herd beef cattle, mainly in the lowlands. Other livestock includes chickens, pigs, and goats. The country has begun to export some of its meat products.

Fishing and Forestry

Ecuador's coastal waters provide a rich fishing ground. Catches include sardines, mackerel, tuna, herring, and anchovies. Shrimp fishing and farming are especially lucrative and provide one of Ecuador's leading exports. In addition, portions of fish catches are canned and exported.

Ecuador's forestland also holds great potential as a natural resource. The nation's vast tropical jungle contains more than two thousand different kinds of trees. They include valuable cedar, walnut, redwood, and brazilwood. The rugged terrain makes the trees difficult to harvest, however. In addition, environmental concerns exist about protecting rare and endangered species of plants and animals that live in the jungle, especially in El Oriente. Deforestation and erosion are also issues in the sierra.

Nevertheless, logging and harvesting continues to be an important Ecuadorian industry. Most of the cut wood is burned for fuel, particularly in the highlands where it is often cold at night. But some woods are exported or used for building or other products. For example, Ecuador is the globe's main exporter of balsa—the lightest wood in the world. Fast-growing eucalyptus trees provide both fuel and useful building material in the sierra. Ecuadorian workers weave together the toquilla tree's leaves to make the popular brimmed straw hats known as panama hats. Mahogany, rubber trees, and cinchona (the source of the anti-malaria drug quinine) trees produce other important goods.

Visit www.vgsbooks.com for links to websites with additional information about Ecuador's economy.

Energy

Energy production, construction, and transportation also contribute to Ecuador's GDP and employ its workers. Electrical capacity has increased greatly in recent decades. So has demand for energy, however, and demand still exceeds supply. Several state-owned energy companies coordinate the production and distribution of electrical power. Private companies also serve the major urban areas of Guayaquil and Quito.

Ecuador's rivers give the nation great potential to generate hydro-electricity (water-created energy). While the country has not yet fully harnessed that potential, it has made great strides. Depending on conditions, approximately 45 to 70 percent of Ecuador's electricity comes from hydropower. This figure represents a significant increase from about 22 percent in the 1990s. The government aims eventually to produce 80 percent of the nation's electricity through hydropower. But challenges such as periodic drought, mudslides, and spotty maintenance threaten to disrupt a consistent supply of hydroelectricity. During the nation's dry season, power shortages and outages are common.

The remainder of Ecuador's energy comes mostly from thermal (heat-powered) plants that burn petroleum or coal. The country also has natural gas reserves, but they remain largely untapped.

⊙ Transportation

Ecuador has more than 25,000 miles (40,234 km) of roads, many of which are unpaved. The Pan-American Highway extends north to south through the sierra. It is one of the most important and highly traveled routes in the country. (The Pan-American Highway runs north from Alaska all the way to the southern tip of Chile.) Other major roads

A biker takes a break to admire the view along a stretch of the Pan-American Highway that passes through Ecuador.

crisscross the Costa, connecting cities and towns. Few major routes cut through El Oriente's thick jungles, but one highway runs from north to south, east of the Andes. Many Ecuadorians have cars, but buses are also a common way to travel between Ecuador's cities.

Due to the nation's rugged terrain, air transportation is vitally important to Ecuador. In addition to modern international airports at Quito and Guayaquil, many smaller towns have airports.

The country's landscape and setting have often made good transportation systems hard to build and maintain. The Guayaquil-Quito Railway, begun in 1897, took nine difficult years to complete. The nation's rail network continued to grow through the mid-1900s. At its largest, the system comprised about 600 miles (966 km) of track, connecting the nation's major cities. But troubles plagued the railways. The unforgiving landscape meant that the system needed frequent maintenance and repair. And periodic natural events such as earthquakes and torrential rains damaged large parts of the tracks. Over the years, use of the nation's trains—both for passenger travel and for goods transport—has steadily declined.

Media and Communications

Ecuadorians turn to a variety of media sources for news and entertainment. Readers choose from more than twenty daily newspapers, as well as a selection of weekly papers. A wide range of magazines also fills local newsstands.

Several national and local television stations broadcast in Ecuador. They provide viewers with news programs, soap operas, game shows, and more. Local stations and studios produce many of these shows, but Ecuadorians also watch programming from the United States and other countries. Radio is also very popular. Listeners tune in to a variety of stations for everything from pasillos and other music to breaking news. Other media includes movies, most of which come from the United States and have Spanish subtitles.

Although relatively few Ecuadorians own personal computers, more and more people in the country use the Internet for communication and news. Several of the nation's large newspapers publish articles online as well as in print. The number of mobile telephones is also on the rise.

⊙ The Future

After the oil boom years of the 1970s, Ecuador suffered a sharp economic downturn in the 1980s. Coupled with a drop in oil prices was a decline in Ecuador's income from its principal agricultural exports. The following decades were a difficult period for the nation. As economic troubles including inflation rose, so did social unrest, and political turmoil resulted.

The 2000 replacement of Ecuador's sucre currency with the dollar was unpopular, but largely effective. After peaking at more than 90 percent in about 2000, inflation dropped to more manageable rates shortly after dollarization. By 2008 it was less than 4 percent. In addition, the nation continued to chip away at its national debts. With these economic improvements came greater political stability.

Major challenges and goals remain for Ecuador and its people, however. The future of Ecuador's environment, from its rain forests to the Galápagos, poses one difficult problem. The promise of still greater oil profits often pits businesspeople and foreign companies against the interests of indigenous people and environmentalists. The shadow of political corruption in the past continues to worry voters. And ongoing social issues and inequalities remain. Despite these obstacles, Ecuadorian democracy has survived social and economic turmoil and appears to be stronger than ever. If the nation's government and economy can both achieve lasting stability, Ecuador and its people may reach greater heights than ever in a brighter future.

TUNING IN

One of the oldest and largest radio stations in Ecuador is La Voz de los Andes (The Voice of the Andes). A group of Christian missionaries (religious workers) founded the station in 1931. The World Radio Missionary Fellowship still runs the modern station. La Voz de los Andes offers a range of programming with both religious and secular themes. It broadcasts in more than forty languages and dialects.

CA. 3500 B.C. Early peoples live in Ecuador, as shown by ancient artifacts later found near the coast.

1463 The powerful Inca Empire begins taking over parts of what later becomes Ecuador.

1492 Italian explorer Christopher Columbus arrives in the Americas.

1533 Francisco Pizarro has Inca leader Atahualpa executed.

1534 Spain conquers the region that later becomes Ecuador. Spanish colonists found Ecuador's capital city of Quito on the ruins of an older Inca settlement.

1535 Spanish explorer Tomás de Berlanga reaches the Galápagos Islands.

1541-1542 Spanish explorer Francisco de Orellana navigates the Amazon River.

1557 The Spanish begin building Cuenca on the site of the Inca city Tomebamba.

1563 Quito becomes an audiencia in the Spanish colonial system.

1808 French leader Napoleon Bonaparte invades Spain.

1809-1810 Uprisings and protests against Spain erupt in Quito.

1822 The forces of independence fighters Simón Bolívar and General Sucre win the Battle of Pichincha, gaining independence from Spain for Columbia, Panama, Venezuela, and Ecuador.

1830 Ecuador becomes a fully independent republic.

1832 Ecuador officially takes over the Galápagos Islands (then called Las Islas Encantadas).

1859 Charles Darwin publishes *The Voyage of the Beagle*, describing his visit to the Galápagos Islands.

1861 A new Ecuadorian constitution comes into effect.

1869 Ecuador adopts another new constitution.

1908 Workers complete the Guayaquil-Quito Railway after nine years.

1923 Charles William Beebe publishes the book *Galápagos, World's End*. The work brings new attention to the Galápagos Islands.

1930s A worldwide recession takes a toll on Ecuador's economy and its social fabric.

1931 A Christian missionary group founds the radio station Voice of the Andes.

1941   Peruvian troops defeat Ecuadorian forces in a border
        conflict.

1942   A treaty between Ecuador and Peru ends the border dispute, but
        the conflict costs Ecuador more than 75,000 square miles (194,249
        sq. km) of territory.

1967   Oil companies discover petroleum in El Oriente.

1970s   Ecuador begins pumping and exporting oil during a period of high world oil
        prices.

1980s   Falling oil prices bring economic troubles to Ecuador.

1992   The government grants Ecuadorian indigenous groups the rights to an area of land
        in El Oriente.

1995   The border dispute with Peru once again erupts into conflict.

1996   Ecuador wins its first Olympic gold medal when Jefferson Leonardo Pérez Quezada
        wins the 20-km (12 mi.) speed walking event.

1998   Ecuador adopts a new constitution and signs a new peace treaty with Peru.

2000   The U.S. dollar replaces the sucre currency.

2001   An oil spill threatens the Galápagos Islands' environment.

2002   Ecuador's national soccer team (nicknamed La Tricolor) takes part in its first World
        Cup.

2003   A new oil pipeline begins operation.

2007   A special assembly votes to dissolve Ecuador's congress. Ecuadorians elect Rafael
        Correa president.

2008   In March Colombian forces launch an anti-rebel raid in Ecuadorian territory. Tensions
        flare, and the possibility of war looms. Peace talks follow in the Dominican Republic
        and result in a settlement.

COUNTRY NAME Republic of Ecuador

AREA 109,483 square miles (283,560 sq. km)

MAIN LANDFORMS Costa (coastal lowlands), Andes Mountains, El Oriente, Galápagos Islands

HIGHEST POINT Mount Chimborazo, 20,561 feet (6,267 m) above sea level

LOWEST POINT Sea level

MAJOR RIVERS Babahoyo, Cayapas, Chimbo, Coca, Cononaco, Curaray, Daule, Esmeraldas, Guayas, Mira, Napo, Naranjal, and Pastaza

ANIMALS anteaters, armadillos, capybaras, condors, cormorants, Galápagos tortoises, hawks, iguanas, jaguars, ocelots, parrots, peccaries, porcupines, short-eared owls, tapirs

CAPITAL CITY Quito

OTHER MAJOR CITIES Guayaquil, Cuenca, Machala, Ambato

OFFICIAL LANGUAGE Spanish

MONETARY UNIT United States dollar. 100 cents = 1 dollar. 100 *centavos* = 1 dollar.

CURRENCY

Ecuador's national currency is the U.S. dollar. Government officials adopted the dollar in 2000, hoping to stabilize and strengthen the Ecuadorian economy. The dollar replaced the sucre, which had been the nation's currency since 1884.

In addition to using U.S. dollars and cents, Ecuador mints its own coins, called centavos. These coins come in denominations of 1, 5, 10, 25, and 50 centavos. They are equal in value to U.S. cents. These coins bear images of important Ecuadorians from the past, such as the author Juan María Montalvo Fiallos.

Adopted in 1860, Ecuador's national flag is one of the oldest in the world. It is made up of three horizontal stripes, as well as a coat of arms.

The flag's top stripe, taking up half the flag's height, is yellow. The middle is blue, and the bottom is red. The yellow band represents Ecuador's natural wealth and agricultural abundance. Blue stands for the sea and the sky. Finally, red symbolizes the blood—and the courage—of Ecuador's people in the fight for independence from Spain.

In the center of the flag is the nation's coat of arms. The center of the emblem shows Mount Chimborazo under a blazing sun. The Guayas River flows in the foreground of the coat of arms, with a ship sailing on the river's waters. At the top of the coat of arms is a condor, symbolizing strength and courage.

Ecuador's national anthem is called "Salve, Oh Patria, Mil Veces, Oh Patria" ("Hail, Oh Homeland, a Thousand Times, Oh Homeland.") It was officially adopted in 1886. Juan León Mera Martínez wrote the lyrics, and Antonio Neumane composed the music. The chorus of the anthem follows below, in Spanish and English.

Salve oh Patria, mil veces! Oh Patria!
gloria a ti! Y a tu pecho rebosa
gozo y paz, y tu frente radiosa
más que el sol contemplamos lucir.

Hail o homeland, a thousand times! O homeland!
Glory be to you! And your breast overflows
with joy and peace, and your radiant face
shines more brightly than the sun.

Find a link to listen to Ecuador's national anthem at www.vgsbooks.com.

Flag

National Anthem

Note: Some Ecuadorians' last names follow the Spanish style. The father's last name comes first, followed by the mother's last name. The father's last name is used in the shortened form and for alphabetization. For example, Alejandro Carrión Aguirre takes the name Carrión from his father and Aguirre from his mother. In shortened form, he may be called Carrión Aguirre, or simply Carrión.

ALEJANDRO CARRIÓN AGUIRRE (1915–1992)

Born in Loja, in southern Ecuador, Carrión Aguirre became one of his country's most prominent and prolific writers. He worked for many years as a journalist, sometimes writing under the pen name Juan Sin Cielo (literally meaning "Juan without heaven"). His articles often covered political topics, and he went on to co-found a political magazine called *La Calle (The Street)* in 1956. He was also director of a literary magazine called *Letras del Ecuador (Letters of Ecuador)*. In addition to articles, Carrión Aguirre wrote poetry, novels, short stories, and book-length nonfiction.

HUGO CIFUENTES (1923–2000)

Otavalo native Hugo Cifuentes became very interested in art as a young man. He first explored drawing and painting. While he continued to paint, he also went on to develop a deep love of photography. He became known for incorporating humorous elements into his photos, even when they were of serious subjects such as poverty among his fellow Ecuadorians. His photographs also capture Ecuador's diversity, often focusing on everyday life.

RAFAEL VICENTE CORREA DELGADO (b. 1963)

Born in Guayaquil, Correa has a long history in economics. He first studied the subject at a Catholic university in Guayaquil. Then, after spending one year working at a welfare center in rural Ecuador (where he began learning the Quechua language), he left Ecuador to continue his studies, earning economics degrees from universities in Belgium and the United States. Back in Ecuador, he became involved in politics as the economy and finance minister for the president Alfredo Palacio González in 2005. In 2007 he took office as Ecuador's president with promises for change.

MARTHA LORENA FIERRO BAQUERO (b. 1977)

Fierro Baquero began playing chess when she was thirteen years old. She had a talent for the game and went on to play in many tournaments and other competitions. Some of these competitions have included Chess Olympiads, international events in which she represented Ecuador. She has earned the high ranks of Woman Grandmaster and International Master. Beginning in 1994, Fierro Baquero also began coaching young chess players. In addition, she created a chess foundation in Ecuador to help teach chess to poor children in her country.

OSWALDO GUAYASAMÍN CALERO (1919–1999)

Guayasamín was born in Quito to an indigenous father and a mestiza mother. He was one of ten children in a poor household, and his early dreams to become an artist may have looked out of reach. But in 1932, he was accepted into Quito's School of Fine Arts. He became a painter and sculptor, and in the 1950s, he won an art competition in which he had competed against more than thirty thousand other artists from Latin America, Spain, and Portugal. He would become one of the most important figures in Ecuador's indigenismo movement. He was also incredibly productive, with some experts estimating that he created as many as seven thousand artworks over his lifetime.

IVÁN JACINTO HURTADO ANGULO (b. 1974) Hurtado is an Esmeraldas native. He began playing professional soccer with his hometown team when he was just sixteen years old. He soon advanced to a more prominent team in Guayaquil, gaining a reputation as a top defender. He earned the nickname Bam Bam among his fans for his forceful way of ramming the ball with his feet. Hurtado also went on to play for teams in Mexico, Spain, Qatar, and Colombia. In addition, he has been the captain of Ecuador's national team since 2000 and played with the team at the 2006 World Cup tournament in Germany.

FAUSTO MIÑO (b. 1981) Born in Ambato, in central Ecuador, Miño is a pop musician. He first began dabbling in playing and writing music as a teenager, and he learned to play piano and guitar, as well as sing. He went on to record an album of pop and love songs, and he quickly became popular in his home country. He has appeared several times on Ecuadorian television, and he also branched out into movies with a role in the 2006 movie *Qué Tan Lejos (How Much Further)*.

BEATRIZ PARRA DURANGO (b. 1940) Guayaquil-born Parra Durango studied music and singing in Guayaquil. Her musical career also got an early boost when she won a national singing prize in 1957—the first of many awards that she would win for her voice. She later won a scholarship that took her to Russia (then part of the Soviet Union) to study classical singing with some of the world's best musicians. She went on to become a prominent soprano singer. In her later career, Parra also teaches singing.

JEFFERSON LEONARDO PÉREZ QUEZADA (b. 1974) Born in Cuenca, Pérez grew up in a poor family. But he achieved international fame as an athlete at an early age. When he was a teenager, he won a bronze medal in speed walking at the World Junior Championships in Athletics, held in Plovdiv, Bulgaria. He went on to take part in other international competitions. His greatest accomplishment yet came in 1996, when he competed in the Summer Olympics in Atlanta, Georgia. He won the gold medal in the 20-km (12 mile) speed walk and took home Ecuador's first Olympic gold medal. Pérez immediately became a hero in his native Ecuador. He has also gone on to compete in numerous World Championships in Athletics, including the 2007 event in Osaka, Japan.

BAÑOS This town in Ecuador's mountains is famous for its many hot springs and natural baths. (In fact, the town's name means "baths" in Spanish!) Baños visitors can also visit the beautiful local church or simply soak in the area's natural beauty, such as nearby waterfalls and dramatic views of Tungurahua, the volcano that looms over the town.

GALÁPAGOS ISLANDS This island chain is a dream destination for nature and animal lovers. It offers beautiful scenery, as well as glimpses of some of the world's most unusual and rare flora and fauna. But visitors must be careful to respect the animals and plants of Galápagos, and to follow the rules designed to protect island wildlife.

GUAYAQUIL-QUITO RAILWAY Although it was a source of national pride in the early 1900s, this railway has become mostly a popular tourist attraction. Though the long journey inland from Guayaquil can be tiring, the train crosses spectacular terrain and offers breathtaking vistas of mountain scenery. After traveling 50 miles (80 km) across the lowlands, the rail line climbs rapidly to Nariz de Diablo (Devil's Nose)—a double zigzag cut out of solid rock.

LA MITAD DEL MUNDO (THE MIDDLE OF THE WORLD) This monument marking the equator lies about 15 miles (24 km) north of Quito. Charles-Marie de La Condamine and his French scientific expedition established the equator's location in 1735. The nearby Solar Museum presents information about the cult of the sun, which was important to pre-Columbian peoples in the region.

EL ORIENTE Take a trip into El Oriente to experience Ecuador's lush tropical jungles. Guided tours offer activities including hiking, raft or canoe journeys down the region's rivers, and birdwatching expeditions. Many travelers also visit the region's protected areas, such as the Yasuní National Park in northeastern Ecuador. The park covers more than 2,400,000 acres (971,246 hectares) and is estimated to hold at least 1,400 different species of plants and animals.

PLAZA DE LOS PONCHOS This square is the center of a weekly market in the highland town of Otavalo. Craftspeople also come to the plaza almost every day to sell their goods—which, of course, include hand-woven ponchos.

QUITO Ecuador's bustling capital city holds a wealth of sights and activities. Long famous for its Spanish and religious architecture, the city is full of Catholic churches dating to the colonial period. Art lovers will enjoy the local museum highlighting colonial art (including the Quito school). Other Quito attractions include beautiful city squares, parks, views of impressive government buildings, and the oldest astronomical observatory in South America.

colony: a territory ruled and occupied by a foreign power

coup d'état: the forceful overthrow of or change in government by a small group. Historic coups in Ecuador have usually been carried out by members of the army and are called military coups.

dictator: a leader who rules with complete control, often through the use of harsh methods

dollarization: the process of adopting the U.S. dollar as a currency. Ecuador went through dollarization in 2000.

gross domestic product (GDP): a measure of the total value of goods and services produced within a country's boundaries in a certain amount of time (usually one year), regardless of the citizenship of the producers

junta: a ruling council, usually made up of a military or political group that has taken power by force

Latin America: Mexico, Central America, South America, and the islands of the West Indies. Latin America includes thirty-three independent countries, including Ecuador.

literacy: the ability to read and write a basic sentence. A country's literacy rate is one indicator of its level of human development.

mestizo: a person of mixed European (usually Spanish) and indigenous ancestry. Most Ecuadorians are mestizos.

missionary: a religious worker who works in a foreign country. Missionaries often attempt to convert people to Christianity, but they may also build hospitals, establish schools, and do other community work.

shaman: a religious figure who acts as a communicator or intermediary between humans and the spirit world

Glossary

Selected Bibliography

Blankenship, Judy. *Cañar: A Year in the Highlands of Ecuador.* Austin: University of Texas Press, 2005.
This memoir, illustrated with gorgeous photographs, chronicles the visit of an American couple to an indigenous village in Ecuador's sierra.

Crowder, Nicholas. *Culture Shock! Ecuador: A Survival Guide to Customs and Etiquette.* Portland, OR: Graphic Arts Center Publishing, 2001.
This book offers a helpful overview of Ecuadorian culture and society.

Darwin, Charles. *The Voyage of the Beagle.* Originally written in 1845.
http://www.literature.org/authors/darwin-charles/the-voyage-of-the-beagle/index.html (March 5, 2008).
The full text of Charles Darwin's book describing his visit to the Galápagos Islands is available on this website.

D'Orso, Michael. *Plundering Paradise: The Hand of Man on the Galápagos Islands.* New York: HarperCollins Publishers, 2002.
This book investigates the environmental effects of human habitation and tourism on Ecuador's precious Galápagos Islands.

Europa World Year Book, 2007. Vol. I. London: Europa Publications, 2007.
Covering Ecuador's recent history, economy, and government, this annual publication also provides a wealth of statistics on population, employment, trade, and more.

Gerlach, Allen. *Indians, Oil, and Politics: A Recent History of Ecuador.* Wilmington, DE: Scholarly Resources, 2003.
This book examines the relationship between Ecuador's oil wealth and the lives and rights of the nation's indigenous people—including the role politics has played in this relationship over the years.

Lawrence, Rachel, ed. *Ecuador and the Galápagos.* Long Island City, NY: Langenscheidt Publishers, 2007.
This travel guide presents information about Ecuador's many sights, as well as its history, culture, and people.

New York Times Company. *The New York Times on the Web.* 2008.
www.nytimes.com (February 8, 2008).
This online version of the newspaper offers current news stories along with an archive of articles on Ecuador.

Pearson, David L., and Les Beletsky. *Ecuador and the Galápagos Islands.* Northampton, MA: Interlink Books, 2005.
This wildlife guide offers images and information about the hundreds of birds, amphibians, and other animals living in Ecuador and the Galápagos.

"PRB 2007 World Population Data Sheet." *Population Reference Bureau* (PRB). 2007.
http://www.prb.org (February 7, 2008).
This annual statistics sheet provides a wealth of data on Ecuador's population, birth and death rates, fertility rate, infant mortality rate, and other useful demographic information.

Turner, Barry, ed. *The Statesman's Yearbook: The Politics, Cultures, and Economies of the World*, 2007. New York: Macmillan Press, 2006.
This resource provides concise information on Ecuador's history, climate, government, economy, and culture, including relevant statistics.

Baquedano, Elizabeth. *Aztec, Inca & Maya.* **New York: DK Publishing, 2005.**
Learn more about the Incas and other powerful historical peoples in Central and South America.

BBC News –Americas
http://news.bbc.co.uk/2/hi/americas/
This news site provides a range of up-to-date information and archived articles about Ecuador and the surrounding region.

CNN.com International
http://edition.cnn.com/WORLD/
Check CNN for current events and breaking news about Ecuador, as well as a searchable archive of older articles.

Fleisher, Paul. *Evolution.* **Minneapolis: Twenty-First Century Books, 2006.**
This book presents an explanation of the theory of evolution, as well as information about Charles Darwin and the development of the idea.

Lonely Planet: Ecuador and the Galápagos Islands
http://www.lonelyplanet.com/worldguide/ecuador-and-the-galapagos-islands/
Visit this website for information about traveling to Ecuador. You can also see images and learn some background information about the country at this site.

Márquez, Herón. *Peru in Pictures.* **Minneapolis: Twenty-First Century Books, 2004.**
This book offers an introduction to Peru, Ecuador's neighbor and sometimes rival. As another former part of the Inca Empire and Spanish colony, Peru shares many cultural and historical ties with Ecuador. In addition, some of the ethnic groups living in Ecuador also live in Peru.

Parnell, Helga. *Cooking the South American Way.* **Minneapolis: Lerner Publications Company, 2003.**
This cookbook presents a selection of recipes from Ecuador's region. Cooks throughout South America use many of the same ingredients and methods to prepare meals.

Stefoff, Rebecca. *Charles Darwin and the Evolution Revolution.* **New York: Oxford University Press, 1996.**
This biography explores the life and science of Charles Darwin. Darwin's study of Ecuador's Galápagos Islands and their wildlife provided important evidence for his theory of evolution.

Tagliaferro, Linda. *Galápagos Islands: Nature's Delicate Balance at Risk.* **Minneapolis: Twenty-First Century Books, 2001.**
This title examines the unique habitat and unusual species that live on the Galápagos Islands.

Further Reading and Websites

vgsbooks.com
http://www.vgsbooks.com
Visit vgsbooks.com, the homepage of the Visual Geography Series®. You can get linked to all sorts of useful on-line information, including geographical, historical, demographic, cultural, and economic websites. The vgsbooks.com site is a great resource for late-breaking news and statistics.

Worth, Richard. *Pizarro and the Conquest of the Incan Empire in World History.* **Berkeley Heights, NJ: Enslow Publishers, 2000.**
Explore Francisco Pizarro's arrival in the Americas and his conquest of the Inca Empire then in control of much of Ecuador.

Index

AIDS, 41
Alfaro, Eloy, 28–29
Amazon River, 4, 13, 17, 25
Andes Mountains, 4, 8, 9, 11, 58, 59
animals, 8, 12, 16–17, 18, 25, 32, 43,
    61; alpacas, 16, 80; condors, 16–17,
    69; tortoises, 12, 17
arts and crafts, 19, 38, 51–52, 70, 71,
    72
Atahualpa, 23–24
Audiencia of Quito, 25–26

bananas, 30, 60, 61
Baños, 72
Battle of Pichincha, 26, 47
Berlanga, Tomás de, 12
Bolívar, Simón, 26
bullfights, 46, 54, 55

Carrión Aguirre, Alejandro, 70
Catholic Church, 25, 27, 28, 45–46
chess, 70
Cifuentes, Hugo, 70
cities, 13, 18–19, 36, 40, 46, 62;
    Cuenca, 19; Guayaquil, 9, 19;
    Otavalo, 47, 72; Quito, 5, 19, 22,
    24, 25–26, 51, 72
clothing, 20, 21, 42, 43
Colombia, 8, 20, 27, 35, 57, 58
Colorado people, 21, 37, 38
condors, Andean, 16–17, 69
Correa Delgado, Rafael V., 34–35, 43,
    58–59, 70
Cotopaxi volcano, 11, 80

Darwin, Charles, 8, 12, 16, 17, 50
dollarization, 33, 65

earthquakes, 11
economy, 5, 7, 34–35, 56–65;
    agriculture, 17, 60–62; debt, 33,
    34–35, 65; dollarization, 33, 65;
    energy, 62–63; fishing, 61–62;
    industry and manufacturing,
    59–60; logging, 17, 18, 62; mining,
    17–18, 58–58; petroleum (oil), 5,
    7, 17–18, 31, 58–59, 65; services,
    57–58; trade, 19, 56–58, 61;
    transportation, 63–64
Ecuador: boundaries, size, and

location, 4, 8; climate, 14–15;
    currency, 68; flag, 69; flora
    and fauna, 8, 15–17, 18, 62;
    government, 35; maps, 6, 10;
    name of, 7; national anthem, 69;
    population, 4, 19, 36; topography,
    8–13
education, 7, 40
El Dorado, 24 , 25
El Oriente, 11–12, 15, 41, 43, 56, 72;
    oil in, 5, 31, 32, 58–59; people of,
    37–38, 45, 46
energy and electricity, 62–63
environmental challenges, 17–18, 32,
    59, 61, 62, 65
equator, 7, 14, 72
ethnic groups, 36–39, 42, 43, 49, 53.
    See also indigenous (native) groups
evolution, 8

FARC, 35
farms and farming, 9, 21, 25, 30, 43,
    60–61, 80
Fierro Baquero, Martha L., 70
fish and fishing, 13, 17, 18, 49, 58,
    61–62
Flores, Juan José, 27
food, 16, 21, 41, 47–49, 60; recipe, 48

Galápagos Islands, 4, 8, 12–13, 14,
    17, 18, 32, 72, 80; books about, 50
García Moreno, Gabriel, 27–28, 50
gross domestic product (GDP), 57,
    58, 60
Guayasamín Calero, Oswaldo, 70–71
Gutiérrez, Lucio, 33–34

health care, 7, 41
history, 4–5, 7, 19, 20–35, 44, 65;
    1800s, 26–28; Inca rule, 5, 19,
    22–23; independence, 5, 26–27, 50;
    military rule, 27, 29, 30, 31; oil, 5,
    31, 32, 58–59, 65; pre-Columbian,
    4, 20–23, 38, 44–45, 51; Spanish
    rule, 4, 19, 23–26, 45
holidays and festivals, 46–47, 54
housing, 42
Huayna Capac, 19, 23
Hurtado Angulo, Iván J., 71

Incas, 19, 22–23, 39
independence, 5, 26–27, 50
indigenismo movement, 50–51, 71
indigenous (native) groups, 7, 20–21,
    22, 25, 32, 34, 37–38, 43, 49,
    50–51: Auca 37, 38; Cayapa, 21,
    37; Colorado, 21, 37, 38; Jivaro 38;
    Otavalo, 38; Yumbo, 37–38
international lenders, 33, 34–35
Internet, 64
islands. *See* Galápagos Islands

languages, 4, 20, 37, 38, 39, 42;
    official, 39; Quechua, 23, 34, 37,
    39
lifestyles: rural, 40, 41, 42, 43; urban,
    19, 41, 43
literacy, 40
literature, 49–51, 70

Mahaud, Jamil, 32–33
mail carriers, Incan, 22
maps, 6, 10
media, 64
Merá Martínez, Juan L., 49, 50, 69
Miño, Fausto, 71
Montalvo Fiallos, Juan M., 49, 50
mountains, 14, 72; Andes, 4, 8, 9, 11,
    58, 59; highest, 11
music, 52–53, 71

national parks, 72, 80
Native Americans. *See* indigenous
    (native) groups
natural resources, 17–18

oil (petroleum), 5, 7, 17–18, 31,
    58–59, 65
Olmedo, José Joaquín de, 49–50
Olympics, 54, 71
Orellana, Francisco de, 24–25

Pacific Ocean, 4, 8, 11, 13, 14, 17
Pan-American Highway, 63
Parra Durango, Beatriz, 71
Pérez Quezada, Jefferson L., 54, 71
Peru, 8, 22, 36; conflicts with
    Ecuador, 27, 29–30, 32
Pizarro, Francisco, 23–24
Plaza de los Ponchos, 72

Plaza Guitiérrez, Leónidas, 28–29, 30
Plaza Lasso, Galo, 30
poverty, 7, 33, 41, 51, 56
pre-Columbian history, 4, 20–23, 38,
    44–45

Quechua language, 23, 34, 37, 39
Quito, 5, 19, 22, 24, 25–26, 51, 72

radio, 64, 65
railway, Guayaquil-Quito, 28, 29,
    64, 72
rainfall, 14, 15
rain forests, 11, 15, 16, 17, 62, 64
recipe, 48
regions, 8–9, 11–12, 14–15, 56. *See
    also* El Oriente
religions, 45–47; ancient, 11, 25,
    38, 44–45; Christianity, 4, 25, 28,
    45–47, 65, 80
Ring of Fire, 11
Rio Protocol, 30
rivers, 9, 13, 17, 19, 24–25, 63;
    Amazon, 4, 13, 17, 25
roads, 22, 63–64; Pan-American
    Highway, 63

San Martín, José Francisco de, 26
slavery, 25, 39
Spanish colonial rule, 4, 19, 23–26,
    45
sports and recreation, 46, 53–55, 70,
    71, 80
Sucre, Antonio José de, 26, 33

temperatures, 14, 15
transportation, 63–64

United Nations, 41
United States, 34, 36, 57, 58, 61, 64

Velasco Ibarra, José M., 30–31
Viceroyalty of Peru, 25–26
volcanoes, 11, 80

wars and conflicts: with Colombia,
    7, 35; with Peru, 27, 29–30, 32
water and sanitation, 41
windfall profits, 59
women, 21, 25, 43, 47

Captions for photos appearing on cover and chapter openers:

Cover: An alpaca grazes in the highlands of Ecuador, at the base of the Cotopaxi volcano.

pp. 4–5 Lush, green fields cover the steep mountainsides near Cotopaxi.

pp. 8–9 A group of volcanic islands called the Galápagos are located 600 miles (966 km) off the Pacific coast of Ecuador. They are home to a vast array of plant and animal life. They are protected as one of Ecuador's national parks.

pp. 36–37 Wearing Ecuador's team colors and carrying an Ecuadorian flag, soccer fans celebrate a victory of the country's soccer team.

pp. 44–45 Students at a Catholic high school in Quito participate in a religious procession. Roman Catholicism was brought to the country by Spanish settlers and is the nation's dominant religion.

pp. 56–57 Much of Ecuador's produce is grown for sale at local farmers' markets, such as this one in Zumbahua.

Photo Acknowledgments

The images in this book are used with the permission of: © Robert Fried/robertfriedphotography.com, pp. 4–5; © XNR Productions, pp. 6, 10; © iStock-photo.com/Alexander Deursen, pp. 8–9; © age fotostock/SuperStock, pp. 11, 19; © iStockphoto.com/Mark Kostich, p. 12; © Buddy Mays/TRAVEL STOCK, pp. 13, 49; © Svarc, P./Peter Arnold, Inc., p. 14; © Pete Oxford/Minden Pictures/Getty Images, p. 15; © V1/Alamy, p. 18; © Janet Pugh/Art Directors, p. 22; © North Wind Picture Archives, pp. 23, 24; © The Print Collector/Alamy, p. 26; The Art Archive/Catholic University Quito Ecuador/Gianni Dagli Orti, p. 27; Mary Evans Picture Library, p. 28; The Art Archive/Archaeological and Ethnological Museum Quito Ecuador/Gianni Dagli Orti, p. 29; © Rodrigo Buendia/AFP/Getty Images, p. 34; © Action Plus/Alamy, pp. 36–37; © ACP/Alamy, p. 38 (top); © Gary Cook/Alamy, p. 38 (bottom); © Paul Smith/Panos Pictures, p. 39; © Julio Etchart/Peter Arnold, Inc., p. 40; © Achim Pohl/Peter Arnold, Inc., pp. 42, 44–45, 60; © Steven Kazlowski/Peter Arnold, Inc., p. 43; REUTERS/Guillermo Granja, p. 47; © Michael Nicholson/CORBIS, p. 50; © John & Jacqueline Wood/Art Directors, p. 52; AP Photo/Dolores Ochoa, pp. 54, 55; © Beren Patterson/Alamy, pp. 56–57; © David Forbert/SuperStock, p. 58; © Santiago Armas/AFP/Getty Images, p. 59; © Max W. Hunn/SuperStock, p. 61; © Gregg Bleakney/drr.net, p. 63; © Todd Strand/Independent Picture Service, p. 68; © Laura Westlund/Independent Picture Service, p. 69.

Front cover: © WILDLIFE/Peter Arnold, Inc. Back cover: NASA